AMERICA
IN THE
20TH
CENTURY

1900-1909

AMERICA
IN THE
20TH
CENTURY

1900-1909

Ann Angel

MARSHALL CAVENDISH
NEW YORK • LONDON • TORONTO • SYDNEY

Published by
Marshall Cavendish Corporation
2415 Jerusalem Avenue
PO Box 587
North Bellmore
New York 11710

Library of Congress Cataloging-in-Publication Data

America in the 20th Century.
Includes bibliographical references and indexes.
Contents: [1] 1900-1909/ Ann Angel -- [2] 1910-
1919/ Ann Angel -- [etc.] -- [8] 1970-1979/ Janet McDonnell
1. United States -- Civilization -- 20th century.
I. Title: America in the twentieth century.
E169.1.A471872   1995   973.9   94-10854
ISBN 1-85435-738-7 (v.3)
ISBN 1-85435-736-0 (set)

Series created by The Creative Publishing Company

Series Editor: Paul Humphrey
Academic Consultants: Professor Gregory Bush,
Chair of History Department, University of Miami, Coral Gables
Richard J. Taylor, History Department, University of Wisconsin, Parkside
Marshall Cavendish Editorial Director: Evelyn M. Fazio
Marshall Cavendish Editorial Consultant: Marylee Knowlton
Marshall Cavendish Production Manager: Ruth Toda
Project Editor: Helen Dwyer
Copy Editor: Valerie Weber
Picture Research: Gillian Humphrey
Design Concept: Laurie Shock
Designers: Ian Winton and Winsome Malcolm
Cover Design: Lee GoldStein

(Frontispiece) Theodore Roosevelt, president of the United States from 1901 to 1909, was the most powerful
political figure of the decade. This painting is by John Singer Sargent.

CONTENTS OF SET

VOLUME 1: 1900 – 1909

Awaken to Change 22
Settled Frontiers • Developing Cities • Unfair Business Practices • Children at Hard Labor • Immigrant Issues • The Segregated South • Communication Shrinks the Land • Change Accelerates

Repression and Reform 34
Restraining Styles • Oppressed Women • From Discrimination to Death • Racism in Brownsville • Early Steps Toward African-American Unity • The First Reservations • The Laboring Immigrant • The Urban Poor • The Plight of Poor Urban Children • Women's Isolation Slows Reform

Mass Entertainment and Leisure 51
Popular Pastimes • Outlaws as Legends • Radio Signals • The Magic of Movies • An Industry Spawns a Town • Camera Magic • Film Tales • Popular Songs and Pluggers • Hot Tunes and High Culture • Entertainment-hungry Audiences • Baseball Booms • Sports in Their Infancy • Newspaper and Magazine Innovations • Newspaper Wars • Magazines Promote Social Change

Roosevelt and the Progressives 68
". . . .this Madman and the Presidency . . . ." • Death Plays a Hand • Big Business has a Hand in Government • Populists and Progressives • Roosevelt on the Fence • Labor Rights • The Wobblies • The Industrial Trusts • Roosevelt Prosecutes the Trusts • Roosevelt Soft Pedals • Promise of a Square Deal• Muckraking • The Food and Drug Act • Environmental Concerns • Public Reaction • A Miserable Job

Improvements in Medicine, Science, and the Home 86
Growing Cities and Crowded Conditions • Americans Fund Research • Public Health Advances • Scientific Advances • Chemical Disease Fighters • Probing the Psyche • Exploring the Elements • Einstein and Rutherford • Science and Improvements in Farming • Home Developments • Food Production and the Canning Industry

The Transportation Revolution 102
The Wright Stuff • A Wing-warping System • The Auto Industry • Auto Mania • From Luxuries to Lifesavers • An Affordable Automobile • Public Transportation Improves • The Death of Commercial Sailing Ships • Inventions Shrink the World

The Arts Mirror Society's Problems 112
Poetry and Portrayals • Sentimental and Serious Theater • Artistic Impressions • Emotions and Expressionism in Art • Americans in Art • Capturing America's Landscape • Photography — Amateur and Professional • Public Art • "To Live in the Scene . . . ."

"Carry a Big Stick:" The United States Intervenes Abroad 125
Imperialism and Anti-imperialism • Conquest Through Capitalism • Controls on Cuba • A New Government in the Philippines • A Man, a Plan, a Canal, Panama • Promises not to Interfere . . . . Unless • An Umbrella of Unity • Roosevelt's Diplomatic Efforts • Tense Times with the Japanese • Strength, Imperialism, and Fairness

A Decade of Change 135
Faster and Better Lifestyles • Working-class Woes • A Nation Expands

CONTENTS OF SET

VOLUME 2: 1910 – 1919

Emerging Modernism: Turning Away from the Good Old Days 150
The Simple Life of the Good Old Days • Abuses of the Immigrant Poor • The Acceptance of Social Repression • The Voice of Social Reform Grows Stronger and Louder • New Labor Opportunities • Counting the Cost of Adventuring Abroad • Growing Hostility Between European Countries Is Ignored • Modern Rhythms and Musical Reforms

Hard Work, Prosperity, and Social Reforms 160
United Women • "On Strike Against God and Nature" • Suffrage Parades • Confronting the Opposition • No Suffrage for America's First Inhabitants • Unsettling Immigration Problems Continue • Bills Discriminate Against Immigrants • Union Gains and Labor Disasters • The Golden Age of the Child • Progressive Education Reforms • New Schools and Colleges Are Built • The Great Northern Drive

American Farmers Develop Production Techinques 173
Rural Roads Help Farmers • Family Farms Struggle • Tenant Farmers and Poor Sharecroppers • Middle-class Farmers • Farming Techniques and Implements Advance • Keep the Food Coming

Progressive Reforms Evolve 181
Public Attention Wanes • Balancing Reform and Dollar Diplomacy • Social Justice Reforms • Progressive Ideals • "Square Deal" Candidate Promises Reforms • An Idealistic Democrat in the White House

Entertainments Shifts from Old-Fashioned Ideals 191
Star Making and Moviemaking Boom • Romance and Pathos • Tent Shows and Morality • The Ziegfeld Follies and Broadway • The Birth of the Blues • African-American Theater • Popular Sports Pastimes

Improving Lifestyles 207
Assembly-line Improvements • Flying Contests • Amateur Radio • Radio's Help in Sea Disasters Saves Lives • Photographs of Disaster Shock Readers • Hygienic Homes and Domestic Science • Changes in Motherhood • A Devastating Flu Epidemic Kills Thousands

America Stands Back as World Powers Align 219
Taking Sides for War • American Employees Gain from European Conflict • American Dependencies Testing Neutrality • Keeping America Out of the European War • Undoing Unpopular Dollar Diplomacy • American Dependencies Struggle for Power • Opinion is Divided Over Neutrality Stance • America's Imperialistic Arms Reach into Mexico • "Pancho" Villa — Wanted Dead or Alive

The Arts Against Injustice 231
Romanticizing Society During the Magazine Age • Light Reading • A Highbrow Revolt • Yellow Journalism Increases Newspaper Sales • A Reaction Against Tradition • Realism in Writing Grows • Anti-traditional Themes of Postwar Artists • African-American Art Remains Hidden • Defining America's New Modern Taste for Life • Free Love and Free Thinkers

CONTENTS OF SET

The War, Patriotism, and Prejudice 245
Arguments for Preparedness and Pleas for Neutrality • Divided American Attitudes and the Presidential Race • Preparing for War in a Surge of Patriotism • Financing the War • Patriotism Spawns Fearful Prejudice • Racism in the Military • Modern Weapons of War • Bringing Home the War • Unveiling the Fourteen Points for Peace Plan • A False Armistice

Peace and Problems 258
Celebrating Armistice • Promoting the Fourteen Points for Peace and Plans for a League of Nations • Compromising Principles to Save the League • Contrasting Responses to the Treaty of Versailles • Suffrage and Prohibition • Modern Values and Postwar Problems

Ushering in the Modern Era 268
Postwar Unemployment and Union Losses • Northern Animosity Toward African-American Workers • Disillusioned Industrialists • Modern Woman Is Freed • Patriotism and Fear • Prohibition Falters • The New Leisure Seekers

VOLUME 3: 1920 – 1929

Out of the War and into the Twenties 294
The Strangers Among Us • Labor Loses Ground • Wartime Legacy: Prohibition and Women's Suffrage

A Time of Intolerance 301
The Red Scare • The Radical Movement • Spreading the Fear • The Fading of the Red Scare • Anti-immigrant Feelings • Racial Tensions • The Rise of the Ku Klux Klan

Warren Harding and the Return to Normalcy 316
The 1920 Election • The Harding Administration • Resolving the War • On to the Economy • The Scandals • Teapot Dome • The President's Last Days

Keeping Cool with Coolidge 325
Silent Cal • The Business of America • The Consumer Society • The Amazing Automobile • Healthy Developments • The Education Explosion • Expanding Cities • The Foreign Policy Front • The 1928 Election

Tough Times for Farmers and Workers 341
Left out of Coolidge Prosperity • The Farmers' Plight • A Search for Solutions • Labor's Dilemma • A Position of Weakness • The Gastonia Strike

The Nation at Play 353
The Hyper Decade • The Dream Palace • The Rise of Radio • A Little Reading Material • Lucky Lindy • The Golden Age of Sports

Changing Morals and Manners 367
The Rise of the Moderns • The Changing American Woman • Feminism After the Vote • The Fabulous Flappers • The Impact of Psychology • Science versus Religion • What's Left for the Moderns?

Advances in the Arts 381
An Atmosphere of Stimulation • The Lost Generation • The Emerging American Identity • The Jazz Age • The Harlem Renaissance

The Problems with Prohibition 394
The Noble Experiment • Bypassing the Law •

CONTENTS OF SET

Enforcing the Unpopular • The Windfall for Organized Crime • The Prohibition Debate Rages

The Big Bull Market and the Crash 406
"Everybody Ought to Be Rich" • The Florida Land Rush • The Storm on the Horizon • The Crash • Hoover and the Aftermath • The Start of the Great Depression

The Decade in Review 418
Isolation and Republican Leadership • The First Modern Decade • Technology and the Rise of Popular Culture • Hero Worship and Charles Lindbergh • The End of the Jazz Age

VOLUME 4: 1930 – 1939

The 1920s: Prosperity Sows the Seeds of Economic Disaster 438
The Economy Surges Forward • The Rise of the Automobile • The Age of Electricity • Other Growing Industries • Faltering Industries • Big Business Keeps on Growing • Political Scandals and Speakeasies • Foreign Policy • Domestic Policies • Prohibition • Changes in Health, Education, and Housing • America at Play • The Changing Status of Women • Culture • On the Brink of Disaster

The Nightmare Begins 452
Hoover: from Hero to "Hoovervilles" • Too Little, Too Late • The Disastrous Results • Relief Brings Little Relief • The Protests Begin • The Bonus Army • Farmers Organize • Vote the Rascals Out

Everyday Life 464
The Downturn Becomes the Great Depression • Middle-class, Urban Families • Farm Families • The Failure of State and Local Relief • Effects on Family Life • Children Suffer • Setbacks in Health and Education

The Depression's Most Vulnerable Victims 476
African-Americans • Mexican-Americans • American Indians • Older Americans • The Uprooted

FDR and the New Deal 489
The Basics of the New Deal • The National Recovery Admistration • Aid for the Farmers • Public Power Programs • Help for the Unemployed and the Elderly • New Deal Relief Programs • Looking Back at New Deal Programs

Organizing, Protest, and Reform 501
The Labor Movement • Three Charismatic Leaders Fight the Depression • Cooperatives and Consumers • The Conservatives Respond • The American Communist Party • Gangsters and G-Men

Fun Times During the Hard Times 516
Games and Hobbies • Spectator Sports • Participatory Sports and Recreation • Trains, Planes, and Automobiles • Reading • The Depression Dominates Writing • Radio: Glued to the Set • Moving to the Music • The Movies: Escape from the Depression • Theater Comes to the People • Art

Pushing Forward the Frontiers: Science, Technology, and Medicine 540
Science Explores the Universe and the Atom •

CONTENTS OF SET

Industrial Research Blooms • New Machines • Advances in Medical Research • The Dark Side

The Final Days of the New Deal 549
"Court-Packing:" A Bold Move by Roosevelt • The Decline of the New Deal • "Americans" First! • The Clouds of War

Foreign Affairs: Prelude to a World War 557
The Manchurian Crisis • Reviving International Trade • Neutrality: It Did Not Work • The Brink of War • The End of the Depression

American Dreams Fade 565
Loss of Confidence • Tensions of War

VOLUME 5: 1940 – 1949

A Shadow Across the Future 582
Rising Fear • Isolationism Grows • The Birth of the Atomic Age

The World at War 588
The Roots of War • Hitler Takes Power • The Road to War • Hitler Conquers Europe • Lend-Lease • Pearl Harbor • America Mobilizes • The Jewish Holocaust • Japanese-American Internment • The Battle Escalates • Battle in the Pacific • Germany Begins to Falter • Dieppe • Glimmers of the Nuclear Age • The Casablanca Conference • Anzio • D-Day: Operation Overlord • Recapturing the Pacific • Victory in Sight • The Battle of the Bulge • The Meeting at Yalta • The Battle for Okinawa • FDR Dies • The Fall of Berlin • The Bitter End

On the Home Front 608
Americans Spring into Action • Productivity and Privation • Rationing • Farm Boom • Labor Becomes Powerful • Gung-ho America • Censorship • Spies, Crime, and Security • Justice and the Supreme Court• African-Americans Fight on Two Fronts • African-Americans in the Military • African-Americans on the Home Front • Rosie the Riveter and Her Sisters • Money, but Little Power • Women in the Armed Services • In Their Place

Dawn of the Atomic Age and the Cold War 632
The Manhattan Project • "The Gadget" • Choosing the Target • Potsdam Conference • The Bomb in a Cold War World • An Atomic Society • Atomic Culture • Control of the Bomb • Bikini Atoll • Klaus Fuchs, Spy • Nuclear Proliferation and Power • The Iron Curtain • The Eastern Bloc • The Policy of Containment • How Real Was the Communist Threat? • The CIA • The Marshall Plan • Cold War Diplomacy • Truman Defeats Dewey • The Red Menace • Alger Hiss • Communists in America

Life in Postwar America 652
Homecoming • The GI Bill of Rights • Economic Transition • Labor Unrest • Postwar Roles of Women and African-Americans • The New Look • The Baby Boom • Truman's Civil Rights Committee • An Era of Power and Abundance

Science Enters a New Age 664
Ambivalence Toward Progress • Military Contributions • Medical and Biological Advances • The Social Sciences • Women's

CONTENTS OF SET

Roles Defined • Technology in Everyday Life
• Inventions for Everyday Life • Important
Scientific Discoveries

The Arts and the Blossoming
of Abstraction 679
American Art Goes International • Chaos on
Canvas • Abstract Expressionism • Calder's
Mobiles • Abstract Architecture • Modern
Dance Innovations • Theater Enjoys an
Audience • Musical Richness • Popular Music's
Heyday • Bebop and Rythm and Blues • A
Literary Plateau

The Golden Age of Media 695
War, the Lead Story • The Radio Lifeline • The
Magical Movies • Women Real or Ideal •
African-Americans in the Media • Journalism at
the Front • Sports

The Forties, America's Pivotal Decade 710
America, New World Power • Anticom-
munism and Abundance • Atomic Fears •
Racism, Sexism, and Anti-Semitism Run
Rampant • The Northern Migration •
Conclusion

VOLUME 6: 1950 – 1959

Setting the Stage 726
Americans: Square on the Surface • Social
Inequities Below the Surface • The U.S. as a
Prosperous World Superpower • The Red Scare
• The Soviet Empire • Communism Spreads to
China • World War II Helps the Economy
Prosper

The Joys of Capitalism 736
Up the Corporate Ladder • Tranquilized Living
• Madison Avenue Influence • Mother's Little
Helpers • Better Medicine • Middle-class Values
• The Downside of Progress • Television's
Mixed Message • Racial Tensions •

The Ideal Family: Myth and Reality 750
The Role of Women • Rigid Gender Roles •
Growing Up in the Fifties • Fads of the Fifties •
A Room of One's Own • Sexual Behavior •
Life After High School • The Silent Generation
• A Young Rebel

Returning to God 764
Religions Grow and Prosper • Catholicism in
America • Religion in Popular Culture • Peale,
Graham, and Sheen • Religion and Civil Rights
• A More Religious President • A Poor
Understanding

Racial Confrontations and Civil Rights 773
"Bloodshed and Mob Violence" • The South,
Then and Now • Boycotting Montgomery's
Buses • White Supremacist Organizations •
African-American Concerns • Other Minorities
• Media Stereotypes

Surviving the Cold War 782
The Witch Hunt for Communists Begins • The
Press and the Public Image • The Cold War and
a Real One • An Unpopular War • Finally, a
Cease-Fire • The Effects of the Korean War •
Meanwhile, More Spies • The Rise and Fall of
Joe McCarthy • Witch Hunt Waxes and Wanes
• Eisenhower and the Cold War • Communist
Confrontations • The U-2 Affair

About the Bomb 800
Negative Views • A Secret Document on

CONTENTS OF SET

America's Defense • The Soviet *Sputnik* • The Atomic Energy Commission • Frightening Mishaps • Clandestine Tests • What Should Be Told? • Voices of Dissent • Atoms for Peace

Hollywood and the Arts 811
High Tech Special Effects • The Big Stars • Women and Minorities • Good Writing • Intense Drama • Intellectual Enrichment

TV's the Thing 822
The Golden Age of Television • Comedy-Variety Shows • The Rise of the Sitcom • Action-Adventure Shows • Quiz Shows • The Rise of TV Talk Shows • Kids' Shows • TV News Invents Itself • Early News Competition • The Impact of Television • Racist Roles for Minorities

Rock 'n' Roll and So Much More 836
Can't Keep a Good Thing Down • Alan Freed and Dick Clark • The Downside of Rock • Elvis Presley, the Tupelo Trucker • Seeing the Stars • Folk, Pop, and Jazz • Berry Gordy, Jr., and Motown.

Ten Impressive Years of Sports 847
Why Baseball Was Big League • Football • Basketball • Other Professional Sports • Amateur Sports

Out of the Forties, into the Sixties 854
Barbarous Allies • A Reevaluation • Paving the Way • Declining Confidence

VOLUME 7: 1960 – 1969

A Decade Unfolds 870
A Backward Glance • A Seedbed for the Sixties

• Integrating Schools • Suffering Heroes • Art and Literature • A Woman's Place • Urban Blight • Ten Troubled Years

John F. Kennedy and Camelot 884
Kennedy versus Nixon • The Bay of Pigs • Waiting for Their Rights • Seeds of Change • Supreme Court Cases • A Crime in the Making: the Assassination • But Who Was Behind the Killing? • Kennedy's Achievements

Lyndon Johnson, the Great Society, and Social Justice 897
Taking Command • Johnson's Great Society • A Landslide Victory • Inner Cities Explode • The Question of Vietnam • The 1968 Election • Another Assassination, More Violence • Stepping Aside • Nixon as President • Appraising the Johnson Years

Whither the American Dream? 916
The Dream Turns Sour • Hispanic-Americans • American Indians • What Role for Women? • 1960s Religions • Getting Around • The Population Bulge • More Sex and Violence

The Counterculture Blooms 928
Underground News • Trouble on the Campuses • Spreading the Word • The Drug Culture • The Woodstock Festival • The Fashion World Explodes • "Turn On, Tune In, Drop Out" • "Won't You Please Come to Chicago?" • The "Silent Majority" Prevails • The Beat Goes On

American Interests: the World Outside 943
A Modern Revolutionary • A Wall and Weapons • Bigger, Better Missiles • Civil Wars • But Whose Land Is It? • The Six-day War • Other Warring Neighbors • Strained Relations • The Rise of the Multinationals

CONTENTS OF SET

Vietnam: War Without End 954
Guerilla Warfare • Troop Buildup Begins • The War and Its Weapons • Death in the Ia Drang Valley • Planning for Tet • The Tet Offensive • The Battle for Hue • Problems for the President • The Antiwar Movement Grows • My Lai 4

Technology: Marvels and Limits 970
The Space Race • War Technology • Modern Medicines • Healthy Food • Guidance Counseling • The Laser • Farming and Modern Technologies • "Silent Spring" • Cleaner Air, Safer Cars • Quality and the Japanese

The Medium Is the Message 983
Televising the Candidates • Top-rated TV Shows • Tuning into FM • Going to the Movies • The Arts Take Center Stage • Art Goes "Pop"

Summary of the Decade 999
Violence and Civil Unrest • The Spirit of the Decade • The Backlash

VOLUME 8: 1970 – 1979

In the Wake of the Sixties — What Now? 1014
Conflict Between Young and Old • Race Relations at a Crossroads • The Changing Role of Women • Middle-class Resentment • Opposition to the Vietnam War

Striving for "Peace with Honor" 1023
The Future at Stake • The War Widens • The *Pentagon Papers* • The Decline of Morale • The Easter Offensive • A Breakthrough in Negotiations • A Doubtful Peace • The Fall of Saigon • The Legacy of Vietnam

Nixon in the White House 1036
Togetherness versus Politics • The Rise of the Sunbelt • Southern Strategy and the Supreme Court • Nixon and the Youth Movement • The 1970 Election and the Politics of Fear • Indecision and the Domestic Agenda • A Dark Cloud Over the Economy • The Right Time for Détente • Parting the Bamboo Curtain: Nixon's Trip to China • The Moscow Summit

The Watergate Affair 1049
The Seeds of Destruction • The Break-in • The Cover-up • The 1972 Election • The Beginning of the Blow-up • The Senate Hearings • On Top of Everything, the Spiro Agnew Scandal • The Battle Over the Tapes • Shocking Transcripts • The Final Fall • President Ford and the Aftermath • The CIA and the FBI Exposed

The Struggle for Social Equality 1063
Following Up What the Sixties Started • The New Immigrants • The Women's Movement Picks Up Speed • Changing Attitudes • The Fight for ERA • Backlash and the Anti-ERA Campaign • Abortion: the "Lightning Rod" • The Struggle for Equality Continues • Beyond the Civil Rights Movement • The Battle Over Busing • Affirmative Action • American Indian Activists Organize and Protest • The Gay Liberation Movement • Equality in Education • Equality and the Death Penalty

The "Me Decade" and Other Social Trends 1082
"The Times They Are A-changing" • The Changing Family • The "Me Decade" • The Search for Self • The New Religious Wave • Cult Loyalty Leads to Mass Death • The Bicentennial and the Revival of Patriotism

CONTENTS OF SET

Pop Culture: Anything Goes 1092
From the Bland to the Bizarre • The Break-up of Rock 'n' Roll • The Power of Television • "Sesame Street" and the Rise of Public Television • At the Movies • On a Literary Note • Art and Architecture • Fashion Plates • The World of Sports • Passing Fancies

A Brave New World 1110
Progress and Fear • A New Age of Space Exploration • Transportation: Setting Limits • Miniature Mania • The Computer Revolution • Other Advances in Technology • New Life Through Transplants • "Playing God" and Test-tube Babies • The Environmental Movement • Small Is Beautiful versus the Global Corporation

A New President and a New Direction 1122
The Ford Presidency • Jimmy Who? • A New Style in the White House • The Focus on Human Rights • The Panama Canal Treaty • The Camp David Accord

A Crisis of Confidence 1130
An Outsider in Charge • The Problem with Conservative Liberalism • The Energy Crisis • The Economic Quagmire • The Rise of Terrorism • The Iranian Revolution • A Rift with the Soviets • Trouble in Central America • Growing Frustration

The End of an Era and the Shape of Things to Come 1140
A Turning Point • The American Dream in Doubt • A Weakened World Leader • Frustration and the 1980 Elections • Ronald Reagan and the Image of Strength

VOLUME 9: 1980 – 1989

Assessing the Seventies, Experiencing the Eighties 1158
Annoying Everyone • Feelings Against Foreigners • Democrats Adrift • Congressional Scandal • Economic Troubles • Reagan to the Rescue • The Nation's Worries

The Reagan Era 1169
From Radio to the Silver Screen • Combating Communism • Conflicting Interests • Nixon in the Way • The Winning Ticket • Surviving a Bullet • Controlling the Skies • Supply-Side Economics, Politics, and Reelection • Foreign Policy • Overpowering the Media • A Distinct President

Concerns Old and New 1181
The Politics of AIDS • Alzheimer's Disease • Guns, Kids, Drugs, and Crime • Gangs Branch Out • The Abortion Issue • Radon and Other Woes • Times Beach, Love Canal • And Yet More Disasters • An Earthquake and a Volcanic Eruption • Artificial Disasters

A Freer Hand for Corporations 1196
The Breakup of AT&T • Merger Mania • "Black Monday" • Savings and Loan Scandals • Change Affects Industry, Retailers, and Services • Agriculture

Islam Ascends, Communism Declines 1210
Terrorism • Communism on the Wane • Following Poland's Lead • Glasnost and Perestroika • NATO Allies Disagree • Grenada and Panama

CONTENTS OF SET

Popular Culture's Strange Celebrities 1220
The Material Girl • Changing Musical Tastes • At the Movies • What's on TV? • The World of Books • Art and Architecture • Television Rules Sports • Consumer Pitches • So Much for Culture

Iran-contra and Other Scandals 1237
Naming Names • The Legacy of Intervention • The Violence Spreads • Fallout from America's Covert Actions • Scandals Everywhere • War on the EPA

The Expansion of Technology 1248
The Home Computer • The *Challenger* Disaster • Strategic Defense Initiative — "Star Wars" • Advances in Medicine • Embryo Technology and Medical Costs Advance • Medical Failures and Dissension • Studying the Heavens • Making Life Easier

Everyday People 1259
A Divided Society • Opiates of the Masses • Televangelism • From Evangelism to the New Age • Self-Healing and Failure to Cope • Public Schools in Crisis • "Not in My Backyard" • About the Homeless • Child Abuse and Teenage Violence • Attacks on Social Activism

The Bush Presidency 1274
Dirty Politics • America in 1989 • Who Was George Bush? • Saving the Savings Accounts

The 1980s in Review 1282
The Role of Government • Religion and Politics • African-Americans and the Democrats • Defense Expenditure Out of Hand • Working Harder for Less Money •

Doubts About Education • The Role of the Media • Starstruck America • Morality and Medicine • A Lack of Support for the Arts • New Technology Means Better Products • The Changing Role of Women • Asian Arrivals Cause Resentment • Family Matters • The Twenties and the Eighties

VOLUME 10: 1990s

Cold War Meltdown and the Death of Supply-Side Economics 1302
The End of the War that Never Was • "Voodoo Economics" Loses Its Magic • S&Ls, Bonds, and Takeovers • Happiness Is a Warm Credit Card • Tired of Turmoil • Iran-contra Crisis • The President versus Congress • Doubts About Leadership Increase • The Nineties Get the Bill for the Booming Eighties • Abortion Divides the Country • The Environment and Jobs at Risk • The Possibility of Positive Change

Honoring Differences 1317
Affirmative Action in Education and the Workplace • Sexual Harassment and the Year of the Woman • The Military as an Equal Opportunity Employer • Prejudice as a Political Weapon • "Political Correctness" and Freedom of Expression • Fair Housing and Equal Credit Opportunities • Racism and Riots • People with Disabilities Make Gains • American Indians Insist on Treaty Rights • A Multicultural Society

"It's the Economy, Stupid!" 1334
Unemployment's Impact on Voters • Labor Loses Bargaining Power • The Economy

CONTENTS OF SET

Dominates the Election • Much Work to Be Done • Rethinking the Budget • A Need for an Educated Workforce • Job Security and Company Loyalty Disappear • NAFTA and the Globalization of the Economy • GATT Goes Forward • Growing Credit and a Leaner Government • An Uneven Economic Recovery

Social Services in Need of Repair 1346
A Need for Health Care Reform • New Health Appointments Promote a New Direction • The Bottom Line: Universal Health Care • Health Risks Cause Widespread Concern • Welfare Problems • Radical Changes Proposed • The Homeless Become Increasingly Visible • Schools Fail to Educate the Young • A Crisis in School Funding • Higher Education Wobbles • Basic Funding Flaws Remain

Freedom's Warrior Carries a Big Stick . . . and a Credit Card 1361
The U.S. Expands Its Role as Arbitrator • Prelude to War • Operation Desert Storm • Inconsistent American Foreign Policy • Intervention in Somalia • More Seeds of War • A Divided Country Dissolves • The "Problem from Hell" • The U.S. and the UN • Europe Haunted by Its Past • U.S. Shares Responsibility, Cost, and Commitment • Global Economic Partnership Encouraged

Crime and Violence Challenge Society 1378
Poverty Encourages Crime • New Drug Problems • New Crimefighters Take Charge • Gun Control Gains Popularity • Fear is Good for Gun Sales • Racism: a Reason but not an Excuse • The Tragedy of Teen Crime • New Crime Trends Shock the Nation • Tougher Measures Against Violence • The Penal System in Crisis

Popular Culture in the Information Age 1391
Couch Potato Culture • News or Entertainment? • Twenty-five Mirrors Reflect More Heat than Light • Sports Entertain and Inspire • Music, the Universal Language • Movies Escape to the Past, Future, Afterlife, or Foreign Shores • Literature Lives and Bookstores Survive • The Visual Arts • Fashion: "The 90s Are Just the 60s Upside Down" • Architecture Reflects the Culture • Popular Culture's Hall of Mirrors

Changing Families, Shifting Values 1407
Nuclear Families Decline in Number • Women Earn Less and Raise Families Alone • Generation X Comes of Age • Demographic Shifts Affect the Economy • Changing Roles for Both Sexes • Inadequate Parenting Hurts America's Children • Right to Abortion Disputed • Medical Advances Bring Ethical Problems • Science Complicates Life • Religious Diversity Poses Problems

Political Trends in the Information Age 1420
The Wake-Up Call • A Lobbyist for Every Cause • Unregulated and Loosely Regulated • Weak Attempts to Control Lobbyists • Volunteers and Grassroots Political Trends • Abuses of Power Create Public Mistrust • Privacy Rights Compete with Public Safety • The Supreme Court Begins to Look More Liberal • Government Tries to Regulate Communication Technology • Packaging Information • Politics of Polarity Shifts to Consensus • Political Battles • A Lone Superpower Looks for Direction

INTRODUCTION

The twentieth century is without doubt one of the most tumultuous centuries in history. This is probably most evident in the United States. At the turn of the century, the nation was one of mostly scattered rural communities, with just a few large urban centers. Nearly one hundred years later, the population is predominantly urban and city skylines reach for the heavens.

America in the 20th Century charts the nation's progress through ten volumes, each covering one decade of the century.

The first decade saw the predominance of Theodore Roosevelt on the political scene along with the rise of Progressivism, which attacked corruption in government and exploitation of workers and children. Between 1910 and 1919, the idealism of Woodrow Wilson was shattered on the battlefields of Europe as well as by the political carnage of the Treaty of Versailles and the League of Nations, from which America retreated into international isolationism. The Twenties were the Jazz Age of flappers, high jinx, and apparent economic invulnerability, itself shattered by the Wall Street Crash of 1929 and the Great Depression that characterized the thirties — a long decade of hardship, despair, and frustration.

The forties were dominated by World War II and the period of insecurity that followed as the nations of the world divided into Communist or capitalist camps. The atomic bomb and the Cold War characterized the fifties, as the first glimmerings of unrest among the country's youth took root, to blossom as the counterculture in the sixties — a time of peace and love, civil rights marches, and, above all, opposition to the controversial war in a country on the other side of the world — Vietnam.

Vietnam dominated the early years of the seventies as Americans pulled out of the war with anything but honor. The crisis of confidence continued as Jimmy Carter wrestled with an economy long neglected and with a worldwide oil crisis. The eighties brought another boom, which turned into recession as the nation entered the final decade of the century and looked to the new millennium with renewed hope.

Many things have changed. In 1903, two Americans taught the world the rudiments of flight; in 1969, two more Americans landed on the Moon and American satellites have traveled to the edge of the Solar System and beyond. Previously deadly diseases have been brought under control and the revolutions in communications and computer technology have changed life forever.

But some problems persist. Children no longer work long hours in mines and factories, but many suffer neglect and abuse, and the perils of dysfunctional families. Minorities and women are still pressing for the last vestiges of their rights. Inner city decay, often leading to crime and alcohol or drug abuse, shows little sign of abating, and in many areas of the nation, the gun still prevails. Bill Clinton, the president for the nineties, promised much. With many grave domestic and international problems to solve, not least among them the crises in former Yugoslavia and North Korea, the seemingly unstoppable spread of AIDS, and the crisis in America's health care system, only time will tell how much he will be able to deliver.

READER'S GUIDE

Themes of the Set

The ten volumes of **America in the 20th Century** chart a comprehensive social history of our century. Every volume pursues a set of common themes, each varying in detail depending upon the character of the decade. Among these themes are:

- Social policy, justice, and civil rights
- Popular culture and recreation
- The media
- Technological change
- Health and medicine
- Politics and politicians — the role of the state
- Foreign relations
- The economy and trade
- The world of business and industry
- Working life and the labor movement
- Literature and the arts
- Sports
- Education
- Family life
- Crime and punishment
- The environment and natural resource development
- Demographic change

In every volume, the role and struggles of women, indigenous peoples, those with handicaps, and racial and other minorities are highlighted.

Organization and Features

Each volume is organized into chapters covering the themes listed above. The first chapter summarizes the previous ten years and places the reader firmly in context, detailing the challenges and problems facing the nation as the new decade opens. The final chapter is a summary of the decade.

Each volume contains a number of unique and interesting features:

The main text in each chapter is further divided by descriptive subheads. In addition, each volume features approximately 100 photographs drawn from contemporary sources such as newspapers and

magazines and includes political cartoons, advertisements, and other important illustrations of the events of the time. In the earlier volumes, nearly a quarter of the images are in color. The later volumes feature nearly 80 to 90 percent color photographs. The maps and diagrams in each volume are all in full color and are designed to present the information clearly and succinctly.

Alex Haley. (1921-1992)

In the introduction to his Pulitzer Prize-winning book, *Roots: The Saga of an American Family*, Alex Haley explained that he was motivated to tell his story in part because "preponderantly the histories have been written by the winners." Through twelve years of genealogical research, Haley sought to tell the story from the other side.

After six years of lecturing all over the country about his search into his family's history, Haley finally saw his book published in October of 1976. It instantly became the top bestseller in the nation, and Haley became a public hero. When the book was produced as a television miniseries, Haley's star rose even higher. In 1979, the sequel to "Roots" was broadcast, titled "Roots: The Next Generation."

Though *Roots* was tremendously popular with the public, reviewers criticized Haley's use of "faction," a mixture of fact and fiction, to tell his story. A British journalist and several genealogists checked into Haley's research and reported many factual errors and inaccuracies. Still, Haley stood by the symbolic truth of his work, and several critics came to his defense, claiming that the factual details were not as important as the vivid, truthful portrayal of life in slavery. Haley was credited with correcting earlier myths about slavery by affirming the importance of family and African culture in the lives of slaves. In addition, *Roots* sparked a widespread interest in genealogy, which was encouraged by Haley, who even donated $100,000 of his earnings from the book to the Kinte Foundation to provide guidance for people researching their own roots.

Perhaps more threatening to Haley's reputation was a charge of plagiarism leveled by Harold Courlander, author of *The African*, who claimed that Haley lifted a passage from his book. Haley settled out of court for half a million dollars. Despite the challenges to Haley's research and sources, his work still stands as a powerful portrayal of the triumph of human will, the importance of family heritage, and the African-American experience.

The captions that accompany each illustration are designed to further enhance the reader's knowledge of the subject.

Interspersed throughout each volume are at least twenty short biographies of the leading characters of the day, with a total of over 200 biographies in all. These include characters from literature, business, science, the movies, politics, the civil rights movement, inventors, and explorers. Each biography is intended to cover their lives, accomplishments, and the role they played in shaping the events for the decade. A photograph accompanies each biography.

> *"To me the worst thing about television is that everybody you see on television is doing something better than what you're doing. You never see anybody on TV just sliding off the front of the sofa with potato chip crumbs all over their shirt."*
>
> Jerry Seinfeld,
> *Seinlanguage*

> *"Not so many years ago, thousands of Americans died so that black children might not be sold anymore on the slave block. Today, these children toil eleven hours a day like slaves. Today, white children are sold on the installment plan for two dollars a week."*
>
> "Mother" Jones

Featured in the margins of a third of the pages in each volume are quotes by leading figures of the day as well as ordinary Americans. All of these pertinent comments were culled from speeches, writings, and other sources from the decade in question. These quotes are backed up with sources and dates, where available.

At the end of each book, the following research tools can be found:

- A Key Dates listing of all the major events of the decade.

- A Further Reading listing of books and articles appropriate to the decade.

- A comprehensive Index of around 500 entries and sub-entries. Accompanying references are printed in italic to represent a picture and in bold to represent a biography.

The Index Volume

In addition to the ten subject volumes there is a 96-page Index volume that includes:

- A General Index of the entire contents of the ten volumes, showing volume numbers in bold, and illustrations in italic.

- An Index of 20th Century People including everyone named in the entire set.

- An Index of Science and Scientists lists all the important inventors, inventions, and discoveries of the century.

- An Index of 20th Century Places shows geographical listings of all the places and hotspots in the news for the 100 years covered by the set.

- An Index of Civil Rights and Social Issues, includes protest movements and civil rights legislation detailed in the set.

- An Index of Women and Minorities includes biographical entries of principal activists and campaigners, campaigns, movements, and organizations.

- An Index of Laws and Treaties with dates.

- An Index of Popular Culture and the Arts, including song titles, books, films, works of art, artists, and performers.

- A comprehensive Glossary of over 200 words with clear, understandable definitions.

- A complete Key Dates timeline, from 1900 to the present day, drawn from the individual volumes.

- A comprehensive bibliography of Further Reading for the whole century.

Contents

Chapter 1: Awaken to Change   22

Chapter 2: Repression and Reform   34

Chapter 3: Mass Entertainment and Leisure   51

Chapter 4: Roosevelt and the Progressives   68

Chapter 5: Improvements in Medicine, Science, and the Home   86

Chapter 6: The Transportation Revolution   102

Chapter 7: The Arts Mirror Society's Problems   112

Chapter 8: "Carry a Big Stick:" The United States Intervenes
Abroad   125

Chapter 9: A Decade of Change   135

Key Dates   138

Further Reading   140

Index   141

CHAPTER 1
Awaken to Change

"We stand on the threshold of a new century big with the fate of mighty nations. It rests with us now to decide whether in the opening years of that century we shall march forward to fresh triumphs or whether at the outset we shall cripple ourselves."

Theodore Roosevelt, at the 1900 Republican National Convention

If the past could ever meet the future, it would have happened at the turn of the twentieth century as it dawned on streets made of cobblestones and filled with an assortment of pedestrians, horse-drawn wagons, and bicycles. A few automobiles, or "horseless carriages," owned by the very wealthy, caused traffic to stop as townsfolk pointed or stared at these contraptions, which, some thought, were surely a passing fancy.

Settled Frontiers

Echoes of the past were especially visible in the frontier lands. Much of this territory had been claimed by settlers under government giveaway programs such as the Homestead Act of 1862, which had offered land on the frontier at little or no cost. During the last half of the nineteenth century, settlement became so widespread that the frontier was nearly

This bustling scene on the Lower East Side, New York City, at the turn of the century shows that horses were still the most common form of transportation. A gasoline-powered car was invented in 1885, and by 1900 there were over sixty automobile manufacturers in the United States. By the end of the decade, cars were being mass-produced using assembly-line techniques.

gone. The American Indians' way of life disappeared with the slaughter by white settlers of the buffalo herds that had been their source of livelihood. Many Indians were herded onto

under the stars or in tents, and whole tent cities had been formed. By 1900, these had been replaced by small wooden buildings with false fronts to make them look tall and imposing.

reservations, often under the careful eyes of government soldiers, while farmers now occupied what had been Indian land.

Settlement of the United States had reached the Pacific coast by 1850, but, except in a few cities like San Francisco and Seattle, conditions almost everywhere on the frontier remained primitive, even after the turn of the century. Ranching and mining provided the main sources of employment and income. Miners slept

News traveled slowly, and when winter came to the mountains and prairies, settlers were frequently cut off by the heavy snows. Disputes were still sometimes settled with the gun, and there were few comforts. Home furnishings were usually handmade and simple. People who settled in the West in 1900 had few conveniences and lacked basic necessities. Only the very wealthy were able to send for furniture, wallpaper, and tableware.

A sod house in Nebraska at the end of the nineteenth century. The age of the pioneer was coming to an end as most of the frontier became settled, but life was still hard and isolated for those trying to make a living from the land.

Developing Cities

Across the Midwest, one- and two-story buildings lined the simple main streets. In some of the larger cities, like Chicago, St. Louis, and New York, three- and four-story brick buildings stood alongside textile mills and factories.

In some ways, conditions in the big cities were better than those in rural areas. People could rely on the mail and sometimes the telegraph for communication. City dwellers could purchase necessities such as practical cotton fabrics, pantaloons, Levis, and cloth diapers at the local dry goods store. Luxury items, such as cherry-wood tables and cupboards, rich silk dresses, and fine china, were only available in America's cities. By 1881, Marshall Field had developed the first department store in Chicago, intro-

ducing new merchandising techniques, including displaying prices on goods and accepting returns. His motto was "Give the lady what she wants."

City families could easily find entertainment by 1900. Orchestral concerts and vaudeville shows were popular weekend pastimes. Although large cities had libraries, in small cities they were only now beginning to appear.

More and more small towns were growing into cities as factories were built, and streams of men and women flocked there from the rural areas, joining the millions of foreign immigrants who came in search of employment and a better life. The American Dream motivated each soul, and many newcomers imagined opening their own shops or manufacturing plants. They dreamed of a good life filled with fortune, of making a com-

These population figures show that, although all cities grew rapidly between 1860 and 1920, the cities around the Great Lakes — Chicago, Cleveland, and Detroit — expanded faster than the average, because coal was available locally to be used as fuel in factories, and good rail and water transportation were available.

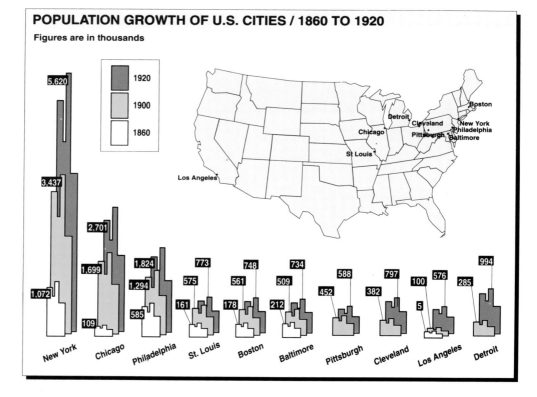

POPULATION GROWTH OF U.S. CITIES / 1860 TO 1920

Figures are in thousands

1920
1900
1860

New York: 5,620 / 3,437 / 1,072
Chicago: 2,701 / 1,699 / 109
Philadelphia: 1,824 / 1,294 / 585
St. Louis: 773 / 575 / 161
Boston: 748 / 561 / 178
Baltimore: 734 / 509 / 212
Pittsburgh: 588 / 452 /
Cleveland: 797 / 382 /
Los Angeles: 576 / 100 / 5
Detroit: 994 / 285 /

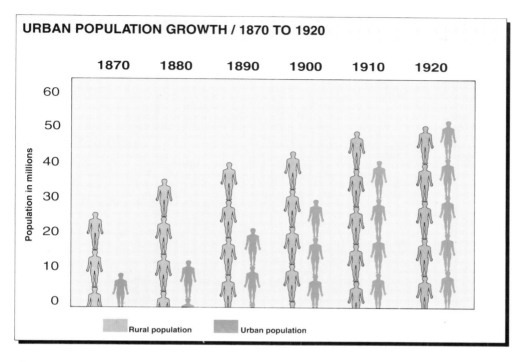

URBAN POPULATION GROWTH / 1870 TO 1920

Rural population   Urban population

This chart shows that in the fifty years from 1870 to 1920, the populations of towns and cities grew faster than the rural populations. People came from the country to urban areas in search of work and an easier life, and immigrants also headed for the cities.

fortable place for themselves and their families.

Unfortunately, economic conditions at the time did not allow many people to fulfill those dreams. All that most could do was follow the progress of people such as John Pierpont Morgan and Marshall Field, and the Vanderbilt, Rockefeller, and Carnegie families, who were busy carving out

The canned goods counter in Macy's department store, New York City, in 1902. Department stores had opened in many major cities, stocking new luxury items and making shopping an enjoyable experience for those who could afford it.

This political cartoon, by Joseph Keppler, illustrates the power and influence big business had over politicians who relied on tycoons to provide their campaign funds. In return, politicians were then obliged to sponsor legislation that favored the strongest businesses.

fortunes in the railway, retailing, steel, oil, and other growing industries.

By 1900, the number of millionaires was over three thousand, compared to fewer than three hundred in 1850. First generation immigrants and hard-working young men found their fortunes in the railroads, steel mills, oil fields, mines, textile manufacturing plants, and department stores. Some became famous from simple inventions, then built businesses around them.

Studebaker, Haynes, and Olds had begun making custom cars, and Henry Ford soon entered the business, too. In every city across the

land, mechanical geniuses and eccentric inventors were designing and redesigning their own versions of the horseless carriage. Meanwhile, wireless radio operators were attempting to send signals across air waves, and the silent motion picture had been invented. It seemed a good time to capture a dream.

Unfair Business Practices

But unrestricted business growth had brought its own set of problems. New businesses contributed to prosperity, but all too often those with

power pursued complete control. The heads of big businesses used unfair tactics to gain the advantage in their fields. They bought out the competition, creating monopolies, allowing them to charge extortionate rates for goods and services.

Corrupt businessmen and politicians had often joined forces during the latter part of the nineteenth century, gaining significant control of state and city government by 1900. In New York City, the Tammany organization stayed in power despite charges that Tammany boss William M. Tweed had defrauded the city out of millions of dollars. Although Tweed was jailed in 1872, the Tammany organization continued to be powerful into the next century.

On a national level, astute politicians understood that campaign funds came from big businessmen who supported any cause that met their interests. Politicians knew their positions depended upon keeping these tycoons happy. Presidents from both the Republican and Democratic parties satisfied big businesses' demands to protect their products and expand their markets. This system of catering to special commercial and industrial interests meant the wealthy became wealthier as their businesses expanded. Often, growth was at the expense of the workforce.

Children at Hard Labor

The poor were hit not just by corrupt politicians and monopolistic business practices but also by the effects of rapid growth in the cities. Housing, education, and medical facilities could not keep pace with the increase in population. Although food was plentiful on crop-producing farms, it was often difficult to come by in the cities. There weren't enough physicians to treat the public, medical facilities were overcrowded, and care was expensive. The cities were filled with tired, hungry, uneducated people, many of whom lived in cramped and unsanitary conditions where disease was rampant.

Poor and immigrant children were often to be found working alongside their parents for lower wages. Factory owners preferred children for many jobs because their fingers were quick and nimble, enabling them to do close work, while their size meant that they could tend machines in cramped spaces. And, of course, they were a cheap labor supply. Children as young as seven or eight often worked twelve hours a day, six days a week.

Reformers were angered by these dreadful conditions and began raising their voices in protest. "Philadelphia mansions were built on the broken bones, the quivering hearts, and the drooping heads of these children," proclaimed one reformer named "Mother" Jones. "Neither states nor city officials paid any attention to these wrongs."

Child labor reforms were slow to come and minimal when achieved. The first child labor law, passed in Massachusetts in 1836, prohibited children under fifteen from working in a factory unless they had completed a mere three months of school during the preceding year. By 1900, only a few states had outlawed factory employment of children under ten or twelve years of age. Thus the children of the working class remained at a disadvantage until the second decade of the twentieth century.

"Why are seals, bears, reindeer, fish, wild game in the national parks, buffalo, [and] migratory birds all found suitable for federal protection, but not children?"

Florence Kelley, child labor activist

"Not so many years ago, thousands of Americans died so that black children might not be sold anymore on the slave block. Today, these children toil eleven hours a day like slaves. Today, white children are sold on the installment plan for two dollars a week."

"Mother" Jones

Mary Harris "Mother" Jones. (1830-1930)

In 1900, Mary Harris Jones was a sweet-faced seventy-year-old who wore a black bonnet to frame her gray waves while organizing strikes and signing miners up to join the union.

An Irish immigrant, Jones came to the United States at the age of six. Long before she took up the cause of worker rights, she attended school and became a teacher in Michigan. When she moved to Memphis, Tennessee, to teach, she married John Jones, a member of the Iron Molders Union, and had four children. Her husband and children all contracted yellow fever in 1867 during an epidemic and died. Although devastated by her loss, Jones went from house to house, tending the abandoned sick she found within. When the epidemic ended, she went to Chicago and opened a dressmaking shop. But misfortune plagued her, and she lost both her home and her dress shop in the Great Chicago Fire of 1871.

After that, Jones took up the cry for better conditions for the nation's laborers, never asking anything for herself. She traveled the country, bringing the message of unionism to railroad employees, textile and steel workers, and miners, whom she called "my boys." She was so convincing that company owners learned to fear the woman that labor leaders had taken to calling "Mother" Jones. Soon, armed guards met her at train stops and tried to convince her to leave town. But the tiny woman had seen many strikes end in death and defeat for her fellow union members. At the scenes of these strikes, she would often be found bandaging injured strikers with strips torn from her own petticoats.

With each strike that ended in violence, Mother Jones worked harder for her boys. She continued to fight for better working conditions, higher wages, and shorter hours well into her seventies. In 1902, she was jailed in West Virginia for leading strikers. When the newspapers reported her arrest, a wave of sympathy arose for the strikers.

In 1903, she organized a group of three hundred mill workers, many of them children, and led them on a march from Philadelphia to President Roosevelt's Long Island home about 125 miles away. Accompanied by fifes and drums, the marchers drew national attention. Crowds gathered along the route to cheer them on. Many turned back to Philadelphia because of the heat, rain, and inadequate food, but about twenty marchers actually completed the sixteen-day march.

At Roosevelt's home, Mother Jones was turned away and told to submit her concerns in writing. Upon doing so, she was given a cursory response from the president's secretary, stating that although Roosevelt sympathized with child labor conditions, wages were a matter the individual states had to deal with.

Later, Jones wrote about the conditions these children suffered: "Tiny babies of six years old with faces of sixty did an eight-hour shift for ten cents a day. If they fell asleep, cold water was dashed in their faces."

She continued to publicize the cause of child labor reform, marching the streets with young children who had been maimed by weaving looms for wages of less than $2 a week. "We want schools — not hospitals [for the children]," she insisted. "We are striking for freedom," she proclaimed, "as the liberty bell struck for freedom."

Immigrant Issues

The government had no policies to regulate wages or conditions for the adult working class either. Talk of unionizing was quickly hushed by business owners, who used the police and state militias to break strikes and dismiss the dissatisfied workers who were seen as troublemakers. After all, the steady influx of new immigrants maintained a continuous supply of cheap and willing labor. The country's industrialists consistently took advantage of their workers during the late 1800s, paying low wages and requiring long hours of work in unsafe and unhealthy environments and dangerous jobs. Some unhappy workers in Europe had already heeded the call of the philosopher Karl Marx and looked to socialism to free them from industrial bondage. By 1900, his voice had been heard in the United States, and some workers were secretly organizing.

Workers whose families had arrived from Europe earlier in the eighteenth and nineteenth centuries felt their jobs and economic gains were threatened by the seemingly unending flow of newer immigrants. They resented the recent immigrants' willingness to settle for poor conditions and low wages, replacing those who had begun to strive for better treatment on the job. Brutal attacks

This cartoon of 1893 shows established immigrants objecting to newer, poor arrivals. In the previous thirty years more than ten million people had arrived. This unending influx of people prepared to work for low wages threatened the jobs and economic gains of earlier immigrants.

and even murders of immigrants became widespread.

Yet the wave of immigrants kept coming. Between 1860 and 1890, more than ten million men, women, and children, most from northern and western Europe, poured through America's gates. Native-born Americans, many of whom were second and third generation immigrants themselves, called for restrictions. Congress responded in 1882 by imposing a law barring convicted criminals, the mentally retarded, the sick, and other persons likely to need public care from entering the country. The same year, legislators passed the Chinese Exclusion Act, temporarily suspending Chinese immigration. But the flow of immigrants from Europe continued into the new century with no end in sight.

The Segregated South

Immigrants were not the only Americans facing violence and discrimination. At the end of the nineteenth century, southern states were systematically legalizing segregation by passing laws that barred African-Americans from restaurants, stores, and churches. In 1896, in the case *Plessy v. Ferguson*, the Supreme Court seemed to take the side of the segregationists when it affirmed the "separate but equal" doctrine, declaring that states could enforce separation if they wished, provided that facilities remained equal. Of course, the policy of separateness was much easier to embrace than that of equality.

Meanwhile, violence against blacks was rife, and between 1890 and 1896, an average of 180 lynchings took place every year, 82 percent of them in the segregated South. The federal government, still with the bitter taste of the Civil War in its mouth, was reluctant to intervene on behalf of African-Americans. So it fell to black leaders like W. E. B. Du Bois and Booker T. Washington to struggle to establish schools and opportunities for minorities.

Women, too, were struggling to make their voices heard above the clamor. Although some states had granted voting rights to women, most had not, and universal national suffrage seemed as far away as ever. Elizabeth Cady Stanton and Susan B. Anthony, who had founded the National Woman Suffrage Association in 1869, still marched for women's rights. Stanton served as its president until 1890.

Women were actively engaged elsewhere, too. Carry Nation took an aggressive public role in the late 1800s. She spoke to people across the country, encouraging prohibition of the sale and distribution of alcohol, seen by some as the main cause of violence and disorder, especially in the frontier lands. Nation later took hatchets to liquor bottles in her efforts to close down saloons.

Communication Shrinks the Land

On the domestic scene, fast rail communication had brought with it the mail order catalogue, with Sears Roebuck and Co. leading the way in supplying goods to consumers in the far frontier and cities alike. Communication had been further revolutionized by the invention of the telephone in 1876. Cables laid across the ocean made it possible to

> *"All men and women are created equal."*
>
> Elizabeth Cady Stanton

Elizabeth Cady Stanton. (1815-1902)

Although she strictly belongs to the Victorian era that preceded the twentieth century, Elizabeth Cady Stanton's life highlights the problems that women faced at the turn of the century. Her efforts and achievements mark the beginning of the modern women's movement in America.

As a teenager, Elizabeth Cady would get her first taste of the inequalities in society that kept women from obtaining any influence. A female neighbor had come to Elizabeth's father, Judge Cady, for help getting enough money from her husband for food and clothing. The husband was spending large sums on horses and luxuries, while his wife had trouble meeting her own and her children's needs. The judge told the woman that, although she had brought great wealth to her marriage, she had no right to any of that property under the law.

Elizabeth overheard, and, angered by this injustice, tore the offending laws from the pages of her father's law books. She swore to expand the rights of women. Interested in the rights of everyone, she became active in the anti-slavery movement as well.

The steely-eyed, heavyset woman married Henry B. Stanton, an abolitionist, in 1840. The young couple then traveled to London for the World Anti-slavery Convention. Elizabeth was not allowed to enter the room because the convention delegates had voted to exclude women. While she waited for her husband, she turned to another waiting woman, saying, "While men talk of freedom for negro slaves, we women are treated as if we were the harem wives of Turks. Freedom for women is just as important."

The woman, Lucretia Mott, agreed, and the two set out together to fight for women's rights. Following the London conference, the two women organized one of the first women's rights conventions, in 1848, in Seneca Falls, New York, "to discuss the social, civil, and religious conditions of women."

Cady Stanton wrote a "Declaration of Sentiments," based on the Declaration of Independence. In her declaration, she wrote that "all men and women are created equal." At the Seneca Falls convention, Cady Stanton called for women's suffrage, or women's right to vote.

During the 1850s, Cady Stanton worked for women's rights and the abolition of slavery, but broke away from the abolitionists after the Civil War because they favored voting rights for blacks but not for women. In 1869, Cady Stanton and Susan B. Anthony founded the National Woman Suffrage Association. Cady Stanton was president of the organization from 1869 to 1890.

In 1878, Cady Stanton persuaded Senator Aaron A. Sargent of California to sponsor a women's suffrage amendment to the United States Constitution. It failed that year, but was resubmitted every year until 1919, when Congress finally passed it, and women's suffrage became the Nineteenth Amendment to the Constitution.

At the turn of the century, Stanton was a regular contributor to the *New York Journal* and *American*. In her columns, she often recommended that women shorten their skirts, add pockets to their clothing, and increase their physical activity.

Stanton died in her sleep shortly after writing to President Theodore Roosevelt, urging him to declare his support for women's suffrage. For months afterward, reporters wrote articles paying tribute, calling her the "stateswoman of the women's rights movement" and the "mother of woman suffrage."

speed messages between the United States and Europe. The steam engine and, later, the steam turbine, had made ocean travel faster and more efficient. By 1900, railways connected the United States from coast to coast, making more governable a country that encompassed so many sparsely inhabited states and territories. Now the frontier was more accessible, new concerns arose about forests and wildlife under attack from lumber, mining, and railway interests.

But for most people, travel and communication were of a more local nature, and the world outside the community seemed vast. People expected their government to protect them from foreign interference, but felt that tackling their own country's problems should remain the government's principal concern. The future, however, was clearly in view, and dramatic changes were in store.

The world was being turned into one huge marketplace. The newly industrialized nations of Europe were jostling for supremacy in overseas markets and American businesses wanted a slice of the action. During the latter part of the nineteenth century, the United States extended its influence over the countries of the Caribbean, Latin America, and the Pacific, sometimes using force to subdue unrest or protect its financial and commercial interests. As the Spanish-American War of 1898 freed Cuba, Guam, the Philippines, and Puerto Rico from European domination, it ushered in the era of U.S. preeminence in those regions.

Change Accelerates

So the United States entered the twentieth century as a world power, sitting alongside the older world powers in Europe. It was also a nation caught up in growth and change, which would spur miraculous advances even as new problems arose. This pace of change would continue at maddening speed throughout the first decade and into the rest of the twentieth century.

Before the decade's end, Henry Ford's assembly-lines would make the automobile affordable to the masses. Early skyscrapers, like the

Sears Roebuck and Co. was a mail order company that supplied a wide range of goods throughout the U.S. With the help of the quickly expanding railways, it was a lifeline for many on the frontier who had no access to large towns and their stores.

Flatiron Building in New York, would change city skylines. The Wright Brothers would unravel the secrets of powered flight, and entertainment would be brought to the masses through inventions in cinematography and radio. Baseball would become the national passion. Women would shorten their skirts and throw out their corsets. Science would uncover the dimensions of space and time. Radioactive materials would be discovered for their medical benefits even as their side-effects would be uncovered. Sigmund Freud and Carl Jung would begin unraveling the mysteries of the human mind.

As technology advanced, the arts would reflect change through impressionism and expressionism. Social reforms would begin, and a U.S. president would receive two Nobel Peace Prizes for his role in ending international wars. The American people would begin to ignore stifling Victorian traditions. They would learn to have a bit more fun, and they would get down to the serious business of attaining workers' rights.

The Overland Limited, *a luxury passenger train of the Chicago and Northwestern Railroad, from a 1910 postcard.*

CHAPTER 2
Repression and Reform

During the 1900s, women who followed fashion wore corsets and shoes that constrained and crushed them. As women took action to gain their independence during this decade, the clothes they wore gradually became less restricting.

The first decade of the twentieth century is often referred to as the Progressive Era. A quick glance at the situation for women, African-Americans, and other minorities throughout the decade shows that while some progress was indeed made, by 1910 there was still much to be done.

Restraining Styles

Women were bound politically, and their dress reflected this. Many wore tight corsets, light kid gloves, and shoes that were usually a size too small. Tiny women were the epitome of style. Many women crushed their twenty to twenty-four inch waists down to ten or fifteen inches.

Women ordered their clothing from Sears Roebuck and Co. catalogues or sewed them at home on sewing machines powered by foot treadle. In the cities, some enjoyed the luxury of shopping in department stores. Men wore derby hats and stiffly laundered collars and cuffs, which women pressed with irons heated on wood-burning stoves.

Only wealthy city dwellers gave much attention to fashion. For most people clothing was durable, heavy-weight, and made to last. Though a few women dared to shorten their skirts for bicycle safety, to many showing even an ankle was considered grossly indecent. The population of San Francisco was shocked when, on August 31, 1902, Mrs. Adolph Ladenburg was reported by the city newspaper, the *San Francisco Examiner*, to be seen riding cross-saddle, wearing skintight riding breeches and a split skirt.

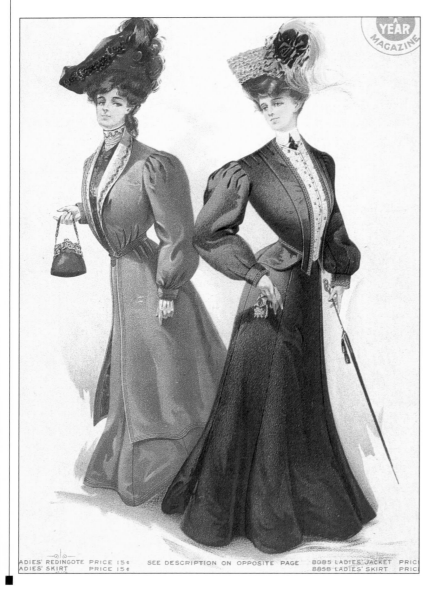

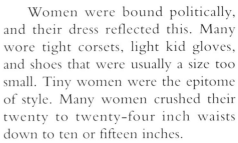

ADIES' REDINGOTE PRICE 15¢   SEE DESCRIPTION ON OPPOSITE PAGE   8085 LADIES' JACKET PRIC
ADIES' SKIRT   PRICE 15¢   8858 LADIES' SKIRT   PRIC

Women processed and preserved their own food each season. They made their own sausage, ground their own coffee, and bought sugar and flour from bins at the local grocer's store. Laundry was scrubbed in metal tubs with hand-turned paddles and hung on lines to dry. In the evenings, homes were lit with kerosene or gas lamps, though electricity was being wired into some homes in the cities.

Oppressed Women

Only a few states, including Wyoming (as a territory in 1869), Utah (as a territory in 1870), Colorado (1893), and Idaho (1896), gave women the right to vote. In all states, a woman's possessions became her husband's upon marriage.

Women's battle for recognition, which had begun the previous century, continued on many fronts. Women who suffered torment at the hands of drunken husbands looked to prohibition as a weapon to fight oppression. The right to vote (which would also have allowed women to vote to prohibit alcohol) was another way to gain recognition and power. Their campaign suffered many reversals and false starts. On May 1, 1903, New Hampshire replaced a forty-eight year old policy of prohibition with a licensing system, which allowed tavern owners who purchased a liquor license from the government to buy and sell liquor. In the same year, the state also rejected women's suffrage.

Women refused to give up the fight, however. In November 1903, after being denied access to the White House, Carry Nation, a temperance advocate who had gained her reputation ripping apart taverns with a hatchet, went to the Senate Gallery and sold miniature hatchets while enumerating the evils of alcohol.

Drinkers found creative ways to "legitimize" their habit. In August 1904, the Subway Tavern was opened by reformers at Mulberry and Bleecker Streets in New York. "Only the purest" forms of liquor were sold there as a way to discourage drunkenness while promoting "spirituality." Patrons of the Subway Tavern imbibed their whiskey, brandy, or Scotch but paid dearly — each drink cost a nickel, and they had to listen to a sermon conducted by various ministers who supported prohibition.

Carry Nation, with hatchet in one hand and Bible in the other, provided the crusading spirit behind the temperance movement. She adopted an aggressive public role, taking hatchets to liquor bottles in her efforts to close down saloons. Many women suffered at the hands of drunken husbands, and prohibition was seen as a weapon to fight their oppression.

On December 16, 1903, one small gain was made in women's employment when the Majestic Theater in New York hired the first female usher. But, on the whole, little headway was made in the women's fight during this decade, though they fought their valiant battles and had their imaginative supporters. In 1904 in New York, the Rainy Day Club organized to give moral support to women who wore "rainy day skirts" that reached their shoe tops. "The short skirt," said Charles R. Lamb, the club's vice president, "is the symbol of the emancipation of women."

Other women's clubs were founded, and existing clubs changed their focus. While clubs in Victorian times had often centered on cultural pursuits, many of the clubs of the early 1900s reflected women's interest in reform and politics. If women chose, they could join service-oriented clubs, which focused on helping the poor, sick, and homeless, as easily as they could join clubs dedicated to cultural studies, women's suffrage, or temperance.

The active roles some women took to gain their independence in the 1900s were a drastic reversal of the earlier roles of Victorian middle-class women. Placed on a pedestal, Victorian women were considered the "weaker sex" and were pampered and fawned over. These middle-class women were not expected to work except to oversee household servants. By 1900, many of these women were growing increasingly restless with this passive life. Clubs that had been formed to study the classics (a respectable pastime for the Victorian woman) were now taking on issues of social reform and suffrage.

But attitudes toward women, their political and social interests, and their clubs were far from those of today. The April 1905 issue of *Ladies Home Journal* contained an article written by ex-President Grover Cleveland suggesting that a woman should refrain from joining clubs. "Her best and safest club is her home," recommended the statesman. He followed this with the suggestion, in the magazine's October issue, that "sensible and responsible women do not want to vote." Women had a long way to go to be equal.

From Discrimination to Death

Women weren't alone. African-Americans had been promised emancipation after the Civil War. They found themselves, by the first decade of the twentieth century, only a little better off than they had been in slavery, as southern states openly discriminated against them. Despite efforts by some in the North to secure equal rights for African-Americans under the Fourteenth and Fifteenth Amendments, many northern states and businesses practiced a much less obvious but equally bitter method of discrimination by turning African-Americans down for jobs, and making it difficult for them to rent or own property.

Since the 1880s, Jim Crow laws, named after a popular character in minstrel shows, were enacted across the South, enforcing segregation and denying blacks the right to vote or to live in full equality with whites. Then, in an 1896 ruling, *Plessy v. Ferguson,* the U.S. Supreme Court appeared to encourage separation of blacks from whites when it interpreted the Fourteenth Amendment,

> *"The relative positions to be assumed by man and woman in the working out of civilization were assigned long ago by a higher intelligence than ours."*
>
> Former President Grover Cleveland

which forbids states to deny their citizens the rights granted by federal law and guarantees equal protection for all citizens, to mean "separate but equal." The amendment's original purpose, when it was signed in 1868, was to provide citizenship and protection to former slaves.

By 1900, groups such as the Ku Klux Klan had prevented African-Americans from voting, using such tactics as death threats, and beatings. Nevertheless black disenfranchisement was based less on terror and more on legal maneuvering. On April 27, 1903, the U.S. Supreme Court sustained a clause in the Alabama Constitution that permitted African-Americans to be denied the vote. Voting rights throughout the state were restricted to people having an education, employment, property, a war record, good character, and an understanding of the duties of citizenship. This ruling underscored the feeling among many in the North that it had been a mistake to try to force African-American suffrage in the United States so quickly after the war. Northerners began to look on discrimination as a local problem — local only to the South.

Southern whites, meanwhile, sought to preserve and expand segregation. Interracial marriage was forbidden, while schools, theaters, restaurants, hotels, churches, and public transportation were segregated.

African-Americans were also kept off jury lists, making it impossible for them to be tried before a jury of their peers. They were quickly and swiftly punished if they were accused of violent crimes against whites, while whites charged with crimes against blacks were often acquitted. Moreover, some whites took the law into their own hands if they believed they weren't getting justice in the courtroom against African-Americans. More than one hundred lynchings of black people occurred in 1900 and 1901. Fifty to one hundred were reported each year thereafter until 1917.

"That was the end of that! Mob justice administered! And there the negro hung...an unspeakably grisly, dangling horror, advertising the shame of the town."

Ray Stannard Baker, *Following the Color Line,* 1908, on a lynching in Springfield, Ohio

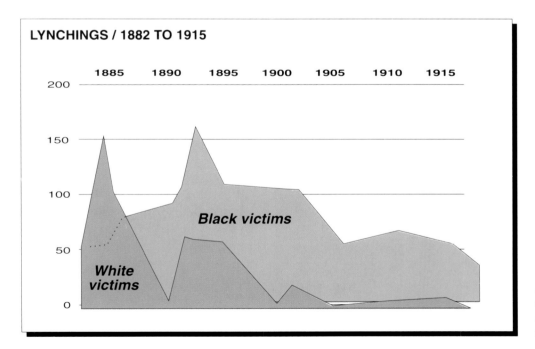

LYNCHINGS / 1882 TO 1915

This chart shows how lynchings decreased from about the time the anti-lynching crusades began in the 1890s.

Ida Bell Wells-Barnett, an American journalist and reformer known for her campaign to end lynchings of African-Americans in the late 1800s and early 1900s, worked to expose the killings and establish laws against them. Born a slave in Holly Springs, Mississippi, Wells-Barnett moved to Memphis in 1884. In 1891, she became part owner and a reporter for *Free Speech*, a Memphis newspaper. By 1892, after three of her friends had been lynched, she began her investigations of killings and violence against African-Americans. Her single-minded determination paid off in the organization of a number of anti-lynching organizations. As the decade closed, she also became involved in the women's suffrage movement.

Racism in Brownsville

One incident points to the power of racism during this decade and illustrates the senseless and unjust discrimination faced by African-Americans. The Twenty-fifth Infantry, an all-black unit, was shipped to Brownsville, Texas, after serving in Cuba and the Philippines. Six members of the infantry were Medal of Honor winners, twenty-six had more than ten years in the military, and thirteen had received citations for bravery in the Spanish-American war. On their arrival in Brownsville, the infantry was greeted with signs proclaiming, "No niggers and dogs allowed."

Tensions increased as the men settled into their barracks. On August 13, 1906, sixteen to twenty men rode through town, shooting at random. One man was killed and several were wounded. People insisted that the black soldiers were responsible. Upon inspection, all their guns were clean and all their ammunition accounted for, but the Brownsville Citizens' Committee concluded that the shots had been fired by the soldiers. A report, written hastily by the military on August 29, 1906, supported the citizens' claims. When the soldiers continued to deny them, an army investigator responded, "Black soldiers are much more aggressive . . . on the social equality question."

A military trial found the soldiers guilty. A shocked President Roosevelt ordered an additional

Ida Bell Wells-Barnett campaigned to end lynchings of African-Americans by whites who took the law into their own hands. From the 1890s on, she worked to expose the killings and establish laws against them. Eventually a number of anti-lynching organizations were formed, but the murders continued well into the twentieth century.

investigation, which came to a similar verdict. On January 15, 1907, 167 African-American soldiers were dishonorably discharged. They were denied pensions and the opportunity to rejoin the army or work for the government. Their names would not be cleared until 1972.

Early Steps Toward African–American Unity

The wave of spirited unity needed to fight and win the Civil War was diminishing as African-Americans faced these kinds of obstacles in their search for equal rights after the war. But some leaders, even those with strongly differing views on how to solve these problems, would not let hope die. Many focused their efforts on education in order to get ahead. By 1901, thirty thousand African-

Americans were educators, and 1.5 million black children and young people were enrolled in school.

Booker T. Washington, a teacher and reformer, encouraged African-Americans to demonstrate character through hard work and thrift. He developed the Tuskegee Institute in Alabama, an industrial and agricultural school. Washington said he was willing to tolerate separation of the races in order to concentrate on economic improvement for African-Americans. Washington laid out his views in a speech in 1895, which is referred to as the Atlanta Compromise. He said, "In all things that are purely social we can be as separate as the fingers, yet one as the hand in all things essential to mutual progress."

In 1901, Washington was invited by Roosevelt to dine at the White House. But this bold move, which earned the president the hatred of

The Tuskegee Institute, shown here in 1910, was set up by Booker T. Washington to train African-Americans in trades that would give them financial stability. Despite their training, these young cabinet makers could expect to earn less than half the pay of white workers in similar jobs.

many southern whites, did little to enhance the position of African-Americans during the Roosevelt administration. Bitter hostility to African-Americans who protested discrimination led to violent race riots in Atlanta, Georgia, in 1906, and in Springfield, Illinois, in 1908. The beatings, lynchings, and discrimination continued.

"The agitation of questions of social equality is the extremest folly."

Booker T. Washington. Speech at the Cotton States Exposition in Atlanta, 1895

Booker T. Washington (seated, left front) and a group of associates at the Tuskegee Institute, 1906.

Booker T. Washington. (1856-1915)

Booker T. Washington was born to parents of modest means in Franklin County, Virginia, where his family settled after the Civil War. As a young boy, he took jobs first in a salt furnace, then in a coal mine, and learned to read at night. While Washington was working in the mines, he heard about a school in Hampton where African-Americans could learn farming or a trade. With little money in his pockets, he left home almost immediately, walking nearly five hundred miles to pursue his dream. After graduating from school in Hampton, Washington went to rural Alabama and opened his own school in a church basement with $2,000 and forty students. The school, Tuskegee Institute, soon became famous for its vocational education programs.

During the late 1800s, Washington spoke to audiences around the country about the problems African-Americans faced after emancipation from slavery. He worked hard to help people solve these problems, but, unlike others who fought for full integration, he believed that blacks should be equal but have separate facilities. Washington argued for industrial education to teach African-Americans trades and to encourage them to go into businesses in order to gain financial stability. He explained his goals for blacks in his biography, *Up From Slavery*.

Washington also owned and supported many African-American newspapers around the country. His dedication to black-owned businesses led to the founding in 1900 of the National Negro Business League to help black business firms to prosper. In 1907, Washington collected the stories of successful African-American entrepreneurs in his book, *The Negro in Business*. A shrewd political leader, Washington advised many presidents, including Theodore Roosevelt, who invited the educator to dine at the White House in 1901 along with members of Congress and legislators.

But Washington was criticized throughout his life for attempting to please both blacks and whites and for avoiding any issues that would cause controversy in the South. His viewpoints came under attack by historian and sociologist, W. E. B. Du Bois, who believed that America's blacks should fight for full equality. However, unknown to many of his critics, Washington secretly granted funds to help fight segregation in the nation's courts. Although his influence declined when Du Bois and the NAACP began new efforts to fight for full equality under the Constitution, Washington remained a powerful leader until his death in 1915.

W. E. B. Du Bois. (1868-1963)

Born in Great Barrington, Massachusetts, and educated at Fisk University, Harvard University, and the University of Berlin, William Edward Burghardt Du Bois received a doctorate degree and lived a life that most African-Americans were denied in his lifetime.

Du Bois' teachers recognized his great intellect and encouraged him to take college preparatory classes in high school. When he graduated, he gave the high school graduation speech, which was a statement supporting integration. Du Bois went on to teach at universities in Pennsylvania, Ohio, and Georgia.

In addition to his lecturing, he wrote *The Souls of Black Folk*, published in 1903, which encouraged the education of African-Americans to enable them to make a living, but also to give them the knowledge and character to teach others. Du Bois' ideas can be contrasted with another great black leader of that time, Booker T. Washington. Washington believed in "separate but equal" status for blacks and believed they should receive industrial education so they could get better jobs. But "education must not simply teach work," wrote Du Bois. "It must teach life."

In *The Souls of Black Folk*, Du Bois' essay entitled "Of Mr. Booker T. Washington," pointed out the damage caused by segregation. Du Bois insisted on upholding three principles: "the right to vote, civic equality, and the education of youth according to ability." The book gave new heart and hope to African-Americans, who faced an increasingly violent response to their struggles to get ahead.

In 1905, Du Bois organized a group of African-American professional men into the Niagara Movement to encourage black education, to achieve immediate integration, and to help the less fortunate. In 1909, these organized citizens and white liberals became the National Association for the Advancement of Colored People (NAACP).

Du Bois recognized that he had been fortunate to grow up in a region of the country where blacks were better treated than elsewhere, especially when compared to the Irish paper mill workers. "In the ordinary social affairs of the village — Sunday school with its picnics and festivals; the temporary skating rink in the town hall; the coasting in crowds on all the hills — in all of these, I took part with no thought of discrimination on the part of my fellows, for that I would have been the first to notice," he wrote in his autobiography.

W. E. B. Du Bois, an educator who had earned his doctorate in history from Harvard, was more militant than many African-Americans of the time. He believed blacks should press for full equality and receive the classical and professional training necessary to become leaders. In 1905, Du Bois and a small group of African-American intellectuals met in Niagara Falls, Canada. There, they formulated their demands and established a plan for achieving them. The Niagara Movement grew, with the support and financial backing of white liberals, to become the National Association for the Advancement of Colored People in 1909, dedicated to fight for racial equality. Rejecting violence, the NAACP relied on legal action, education, peaceful protests, and voter participation to gain equality. Du Bois and Washington continued to

"There is only one sure basis of social reform, and that is truth — a careful, detailed knowledge of the essential facts of each social problem."

W. E. B. Du Bois

disagree about the breadth of rights blacks should fight to achieve at the same time that they worked diligently to improve their race's economic and educational conditions.

One area in which African-Americans did get a fair chance was when land was parceled and homesteaded on America's western frontier. In July 1904, 382,000 acres of government land on the Rosebud Reservation in South Dakota were parceled into 160-acre settlements. More than thirty thousand people of all races came on the Chicago and Northwestern Railroad to the opening in order to stake a claim. This was an exception, however, and, on the whole, African-Americans continued at a disadvantage throughout

the decade. Even by 1910, black workers earned, on average, one-third of the pay of white workers.

The First Reservations

Part of the reason the frontier lands and other parts of the country were open for settlement was because the original American Indian inhabitants had been removed from the land by death, disease, or under the threat of attack by the military or by European-American settlers. For example, with the discovery of gold in the 1860s, miners and prospectors invaded the Apache homeland, claiming the lands as their own. The U.S. Army moved in, building forts to

Many American Indians, such as this Sioux family, were rounded up, placed on reservations, and forced into new economic and social structures. Often badly treated and deprived of adequate food, clothing, and education, they lost their own customs and culture. Despair led many to alcohol and drug abuse.

Geronimo. (1829-1909)

Born in a camp near the headwaters of the Gila River in what is now Arizona, the Apache Indian baby was named "Goyahkla," meaning "One Who Yawns." Of his early life, Geronimo said, "This range is our fatherland. Among these mountains our wigwams were hidden; the scattered valleys contained our fields; the boundless prairies, stretching away on every side, were our pastures; the rocky caverns were our burial places."

The Apaches hunted deer, antelope, and elk, and gathered wild fruits and vegetables. They were fierce warriors, stealing horses, food, and cattle to meet their needs, and attacking Mexicans, neighboring Indian groups, and white settlers in order to defend their land.

Geronimo learned the skills necessary for his survival at his father's knee. He made bows and arrows, ran long distances, and hunted for food as a child. To train for war, he wrestled, dodged lances, hid and learned to track animals.

As Geronimo grew to manhood, he took a wife, a tall, slender girl named Alope who bore three children. The family lived the traditional Indian way of life.

When the United States took possession of Arizona in 1848, after the Mexican-American War, the Apache warriors began raiding American surveyors' camps, killing the men, women, and children who came with them.

Sometime during the 1850s, the camp where Geronimo and his family lived was attacked while the warriors were out hunting. Geronimo set out for revenge. He led a band of rebels on attack after attack during the 1850s and 1860s. Before long, they were the most feared band of rebels along the Mexican border.

When the remaining Apaches were moved to the San Carlos Reservation, Geronimo refused to live there. He continued to attack settlers and hid out in the mountains. He and his band were captured again and again but always escaped.

Finally, in the late summer of 1886, Geronimo was captured and promised "I will quit the warpath and live in peace hereafter." He was exiled to Fort Pickens, Florida, until 1887, when he was reunited with his family. In 1893, Geronimo and his family were moved to a reservation at Fort Sills, Oklahoma, where he grew food on a small farm.

Because he was a living example of America's history, many tourists stopped to see the stern warrior who sat at the reservation's gate. He made a plea to any who would listen: "Do what you like with me, but let my people go home. Let them live in peace in the land of their fathers."

Sometimes he would sell autographs and handmade bows and arrows to tourists. Fair committees would regularly request that the then Indian Bureau in Washington delegate a group of American Indians to come to their fairs. Geronimo was often chosen to represent the Apaches. He was held up by white Americans as an example of the fierce determination of America's native people to remain free. At each fair, he repeated his plea that his people be allowed to return to the desert and mountains.

On March 5, 1905, Geronimo rode astride a calico pony in President Roosevelt's inaugural parade. He was dressed in beaded buckskin, war paint streaking his cheeks. As he passed, people cheered and shouted his name. Roosevelt smiled and saluted the man who had fought for his people's land. Despite his pleas to be returned to the western region, Geronimo lived out his days virtually imprisoned on the reservation in Oklahoma.

protect the miners and their families from the Apaches.

As the two cultures clashed, raids became more vicious. White settlers became merciless in their efforts to wipe out the Apaches. The U.S. Army's treatment of the Indians became so brutal that in 1871 President Ulysses S. Grant formed a Board of Indian Commissioners to look after Indian affairs. Congress soon voted to round up the Apaches and place them on reservations. There the Indians were poorly treated. They were often given rancid meat, little clothing, and few blankets. The Indians were cheated again and again.

In 1875, the government broke its treaties with the Indians to give even more land to white settlers. Soldiers moved the Apaches from southern to central Arizona away from their homelands. They were placed in the San Carlos Reservation, called "Hell's Forty Acres" both by the soldiers who worked there as guards and the Indians who had to live there.

By this time, many other American Indians had also been rounded up and placed on reservations. Those who fought white settlers and resisted resettlement were taken at gunpoint by the military to their new homes.

The Dawes Act, enacted in 1887, further undermined the Indians' way of life. This legislation divided parcels of tribal lands up into 40- to 160-acre plots that were turned over to individual American Indians to farm. Leftover parcels were sold to whites. The government's plan was to educate Indians using proceeds from these land sales. Unfortunately, the proceeds were not sufficient to fund a quality education. The education that was provided taught the Indians reading, writing, and arithmetic but they lost touch with their own tribe, their own language, and their own customs. Nor did this education help them fit in with white culture; rather it further isolated them.

In addition, the social structure of the tribes was disrupted. The Indians had not been raised to farm, and much of the land was unsuitable, so many Indians failed at farming or sold off their lands and lived off the money they received. When the money ran out, they were left penniless, untrained, and without the community structure and traditions of their tribes, which had either been scattered or gathered on government-run reservations.

The reservations also isolated American Indians from one another and gave them little in the way of the open fields, mountain ranges, and the untamed space they had been born to. Many were saddened by their loss of freedom. They grew restless and bored. The abuse of alcohol and drugs became common practice on the reservations.

The Laboring Immigrant

While women, African-Americans, and American Indians in the United States faced repression and injustice, wave after wave of new immigrants came to America's shores to seek a new life. In 1904, the steerage fare from Europe to North America by sea was cut to about $10, allowing for a further inrush of immigrants. New York's Ellis Island became the main conduit through which hundreds of thousands of these would-be Americans passed. Those who already had a job lined up for themselves could repay the cost of their passage in a week.

In addition, the railroads were selling land located alongside the tracks cheaply — $4 an acre — and giving free transportation to the immigrants who bought it. The railroads knew that settling this land would create new business for them.

The influx of the so-called new immigrants, many from southern or eastern Europe, caused alarm among public and labor groups. They were concerned about the low wages many of the immigrants were prepared to accept for their work. In 1905, Roosevelt struck out at the critics of his immigration policy in a December 5 speech to Congress. He said, "There is no danger in having too many immigrants of the right kind." By the right kind, he meant those willing to undergo Americanization — to learn English, embrace the values and customs of the middle class, work hard in their profession, obey the law, and improve themselves through education.

By 1907, the foreign born made up 14 percent of the population but 50 percent of the labor force. "Cheap labor, ignorant labor, takes our jobs and cuts our wages," complained the

An Italian family arrives on Ellis Island in this Lewis Hine photograph. In 1900, Italian immigrants accounted for one hundred thousand new arrivals, as opposed to just twelve thousand in 1880. Southern Europeans were paid less than northern Europeans and were seen by some as bringing an inferior culture to the country.

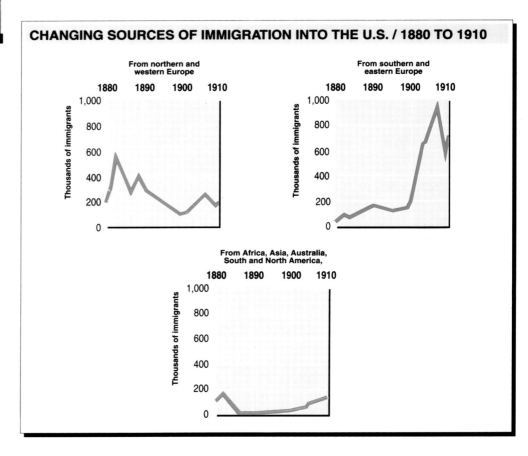

CHANGING SOURCES OF IMMIGRATION INTO THE U.S. / 1880 TO 1910

From northern and western Europe

From southern and eastern Europe

From Africa, Asia, Australia, South and North America,

All through the second half of the nineteenth century, most immigrants to the U.S. came from northern and western Europe. At the end of the century a significant change took place, as large numbers of people from southern and eastern Europe arrived and continued to do so for nearly twenty years.

"[The foreign born are but] accretions of simple people who carry in their hearts a desire for mere goodness."

Jane Addams

president of the American Federation of Labor, Samuel Gompers. To some extent, this was true. Though subsistence wages stood at around $745 a year, immigrant wages ranged from $722 for Swedes to as low as $400 for southern Italians and Hungarians.

Some, like zoologist H. F. Osborn, felt threatened by the influx of so many Slavs, Slovaks, Serbs, Croats, Bosnians, and Herzegovinians, many of whom were Catholic or Jewish. Osborn proclaimed the primary task of the nation should be "the conservation and multiplication for our country of the best spiritual, moral, intellectual and physical forces of heredity."

Reformers like Jane Addams felt differently. Her work in the immigrant ghettos went on regardless of

the nationality of the poor. She continued to believe that the United States should remain Thomas Paine's "asylum for mankind."

Addams, together with Ellen Gates Starr, had founded a shelter for Chicago's homeless called Hull House in 1889. Later, she also founded Settlement House, a neighborhood center that offered day care and college courses for people of every race and national heritage. Addams organized civic groups to push for labor and housing reforms for women and children. This reformer, whose heart ached over the plight of poor children, helped set up the first juvenile court, and in 1909, she was elected the first woman president of the National Conference of Charities and Corrections. Addams and Starr stressed the need for a more equitable distribution of income between the rich and poor. Addams quoted Saint Augustine: "Thou givest bread to the hungry, but better were it, that none hungered and thou had'st none to give him."

Under pressure, Roosevelt formed a presidential panel on immigration in February 1907, and in March, the Immigration Act made it possible for immigrants without U.S. passports to be barred from entry to the country if it was deemed detrimental to American labor conditions. In March 1910, the act was amended by Congress to bar paupers, criminals, anarchists, and diseased persons from entering the country.

The Urban Poor

Most immigrants settled into the already overcrowded cities, where there were jobs to be found. Their swelling numbers added to the already overwhelming city populations. Many of the jobs for the immigrants and the existing poor alike were so badly paid that city dwellers turned to other ways of making money. In 1906, the number of prostitutes in Chicago was estimated at ten thousand. Gambling, extortion, and robbery were commonplace. So were drug addiction and violence.

Housing and sanitation were inadequate, garbage and sewage piled up in the streets, and poor families

Sweatshops, like this one in New York City, provided poorly paid jobs for newly arrived immigrants. Labor groups and earlier immigrants feared that such cheap labor would force their own wages down.

Cities were already over-crowded at the turn of the century, and immigrants were still arriving in huge numbers. Housing and sanitation were inadequate, and poor families often lived in one room. Others built shantytowns like these on any empty lot they could find.

often lived in just one room. Landlords converted garages, storage shacks, and even stables into apartments. The stench of rotten garbage was terrible, but worse still were the rats, insects, and germs that thrived on the garbage piles.

At the bottom of the social heap were the African-Americans. They were forced by the white majority to live in just small parts of most cities; these neighborhoods became even more crowded as their numbers swelled.

Far from helping the urban poor, many politicians sought to benefit from their poverty. To keep themselves in power, city officials bribed the poor city dwellers, especially the immigrants and the African-Americans, buying votes in exchange for jobs, legal advice, or even a bag of coal.

The Plight of Poor Urban Children

Jane Addams (1860-1935) founded a settlement house for the poor, Hull House in Chicago, in 1889. It contained a boarding house, dispensary, nursery, school, and art gallery. Later, she crusaded for child labor reform, women's suffrage, and international peace.

Child workers fared little better during the decade. Young children worked in factories, sweatshops, and even down in coal mines. In 1903, the labor leader "Mother" Jones led a small army of children on a march to

New York to protest about the employment and exploitation of children. At that time, around 1.5 million children in the United States worked for as little as 25 cents a day. Roosevelt refused to meet the marchers.

In 1912, however, the Federal Children's Bureau would finally open its doors after years of lobbying by children's rights activists like Lillian Wald. It had taken years to organize the bureau simply because children were not a priority and other matters came first for the country's bureaucrats. It would not be until 1916 that the first child labor law would be passed by Congress. This set a minimum age and an eight-hour workday for children working in companies involved in interstate and foreign commerce.

Women's Isolation Slows Reform

Although progress in the granting of rights to children, women, and minorities had been stymied for the most part during this decade, leaders of the different movements had become more organized. Laws to protect minorities and give them equal opportunities were also given some consideration, although far-reaching federal civil rights laws wouldn't be passed until the mid-sixties. The women's movement had furthered prohibition and women's suffrage, both of which would become law in the next two decades.

Even by the closing years of the

These boys are working at midnight in an Indiana glassworks. It was common for children to work in factories and mines, and even six-year-olds worked eight-hour shifts. Despite President Roosevelt's reputation as a progressive president, he did little to prevent the exploitation of children as cheap labor. Photographs like this one by Lewis Hine were used to promote reform.

In 1900, women had no possessions of their own upon marriage and no political rights in most states. The decade saw no changes in the law. However, many thousands of women had joined suffrage groups during the 1890s.

"We may discount all the scare headlines about what will happen if women do thus and so. They have done nearly everything, and the heavens have not fallen."

Ellen Richards, chemist, *Woman's Journal*, 1907

first decade, the prohibition movement was gaining ground. On January 1, 1908, statewide prohibition became law in Georgia. The same year, most railroads outlawed drinking by employees, both on the job and off.

Women had, for the most part, remained tied to the home over the first decade of the twentieth century and would for some time afterward, but some gained a little freedom from their workload as electrical and other services were added in city after city. By 1910, the more wealthy households could boast electric lights, indoor plumbing, gas stoves, vacuum cleaners, and electric washing machines. They would gain even more from the inventions developed over the following decades. While some families would gain more leisure time using these new gadgets, most modern technology remained affordable only to the wealthy, who simply handed them to their servants to operate. It would be some time before labor-saving devices became available to all.

Even by 1908, women who smoked in public were frowned upon in polite society. John B. Martin, owner of Cafe Martin, was quoted in a New York newspaper as saying, "I am afraid the average American is still too puritanical to allow the innovation." In 1909, the Sullivan Ordinance was passed, making it illegal for a woman to smoke in public in New York. Restaurant managers were subject to fines if they allowed women to smoke in their establishments. The law did not apply to men.

By the decade's end, fashion experts still dictated that proper women should cover themselves completely. Sheath bathing suits, which first became popular in 1908, included tights and ballet slippers, bloused sleeves, and skirts to the knees. Some daring society women did appear in sheath skirts in 1908 and 1909. These skirts shocked the general public with their form-fitting cuts, making the wearing of petticoats an impossibility. The simple freedom from confining undergarments must have been refreshing in these post-Victorian times.

CHAPTER 3
Mass Entertainment and Leisure

Popular Pastimes

Leisure time during the first decade of the twentieth century was a time for baseball, picnics, and long Sunday drives in the horse and carriage, or, for some, the new family car. It was an era of old-fashioned family get-togethers, which could mean everyone gathered around the piano on Sunday evenings for a sing-along. Phonographs were still too impractical for home use, but in 1903, a small American company issued recordings of opera stars for the few who owned hand-cranked Victrolas.

There was no radio or television

Home entertainment often centered around the piano and family sing-alongs. During this decade, the sheet music of popular songs often sold over a million copies. These songs reflected the events changing the world outside, such as the invention of the airplane and the growing popularity of automobiles. Unfortunately, they also contained examples of the racial predudice widespread at that time.

The St. Louis World's Fair of 1904 was visited by thousands of Americans making use of the rapid advances in transportation. The American Automobile Association organized a ride from New York to the fair, which was completed by fifty-nine vehicles. This picture shows the Festive Hall and Cascades.

to keep people glued to their couches; church remained the center of activity in many towns. Socials were popular, and so was vaudeville, with its slapstick humor, song-and-dance routines, and juggling. By 1907, the follies, shows with music, dance, and skits, were also entertaining millions. Anyone who was anyone in the entertainment world hoped to play the Palace, a famous huge theater in New York City where Will Rogers and Eddie Cantor would polish their comic styles over the next decade.

Around the piano, songs such as "In My Merry Oldsmobile" and "Come Josephine, in My Flying Machine" symbolized the changing times and changing dreams people experienced. Yet painful prejudices were found in some songs, indicating the country's need to work out racial issues. "The Darktown Strutters Ball" and "Bill Bailey Won't You Please Come Home" were just two songs that portrayed blacks as childish and naive objects of fun.

The extremely rich played tennis and golf or traveled to Europe, while middle-class Americans visited their county fairs to see hot-air balloon races, view agricultural exhibits, and enter contests of all sorts. The 1904 World's Fair in St. Louis celebrated

the hundredth anniversary of the Louisiana Purchase and thousands attended.

Outlaws as Legends

Faster travel, better communication, and more leisure worked together to turn the western frontier of the late 1800s into a legend from an earlier century. Communication systems linked the two coasts, and the West was comfortably settled. Those same systems encouraged the spread of cowboy folklore and outlaw legend back East.

Only a few reported incidents of violence on the frontier made the papers in the 1900s. On August 6, 1902, one newspaper noted that Harry Tracy, "a notorious outlaw, committed suicide, ending a 59-day flight through Oregon and Washington. He had escaped from the Oregon State Penitentiary on June 9, travelled across 1,500 miles of wild country, killed six officers and fellow fugitive, David Merrill, while eluding Indian trackers, hundreds of law officers and vigilantes." The newspaper article added that Tracy had stolen horses and robbed farmers along the way. Yet he paled in comparison to those earlier villains, Frank and Jesse James, the two infamous brothers who had formed a band of outlaws in the late 1800s, robbing banks and trains across the country.

Although the lifestyle was still rugged and rough around the edges, it seemed the Wild West was being tamed, as tent cities gave way to permanent settlements. Churches and one-room schools had been built, and families settled down on ranches and farms. Technological changes like telegraphs and telephones, cars and railroads were changing the face of the West.

Radio Signals

Entertainment, like every other detail of life in this decade, would also be touched by technological change and innovation. Although few may have noticed the tiny article in the *Electric Review* magazine of September 1900, it predicted that radio would make vast strides now that Sir William H. Pierce found it possible to convey audible speech for six to eight miles without wires.

While the world paid only scant attention, radio operators continued their quiet experimenting. In 1901, the inventor of wireless, Guglielmo Marconi, sent signals across the Atlantic ocean, from Cornwall, in England, to Newfoundland, in Canada. The letter S was repeated over and over. The era of wireless telegraphy had truly begun.

The telephone was making great strides, too. On July 4, 1903, President Roosevelt exchanged a message with Philippine Governor Taft via an eight thousand-mile long Pacific cable that had been laid on the seabed in four sections.

The Magic of Movies

The motion picture industry was in its infancy as 1900 dawned. Although it would be a few years before moving pictures would be available to the general public, the technology was moving along rapidly. Before the advent of the movies, the primary form of motion picture entertainment had been in penny arcades, where for a nickel, patrons could look through kinetoscopes, patented by Thomas Edison. Viewers watched as celluloid pictures flipped past, creating the illusion of movement.

Thomas Edison also created the first movie studio in 1893 in Orange, New Jersey. It was nicknamed the "Black Maria" because of its design. To create the studio, Edison constructed a large box covered with black tar paper. The box rotated to capture sunlight all day through a removable roof. Vaudeville and circus acts were invited to perform on the stage. Some of the acts that Edison filmed included Annie Oakley and Buffalo Bill's Wild West Show. One of the most memorable of the first short films captured a man sneezing. It was simply called *Fred Ott's Sneeze*.

By 1895, advances had led to the cinematographe, a camera/printer/projector that weighed ten pounds and was powered by a hand crank. An arc lantern was used to project the film. On April 23, 1896, Edison held the first public movie screening at Koster and Bial's Music Hall in New York. His shots of breaking waves frightened nervous spectators.

An Industry Spawns a Town

Change in this industry and the town it grew up in would be swift over the first two decades of the twentieth century. In 1900, Hollywood, California, was a rural community populated by conservative farmers. Between 1900 and 1907, an oil boom would make the popula-

The kinetoscope was the first motion picture entertainment, available to all in penny arcades. Pictures moved past the viewer's eyes at the rate of forty photographs per second, creating an impression of movement. Thomas Edison, its inventor, created the first movie studio in 1893.

Thomas Alva Edison. (1847-1931)

The "Wizard of Menlo Park" spent less than three months in formal school. Edison's mother removed him and taught him at home after the schoolmaster told his mother the boy was "addled." Yet he changed the lives of millions with his many inventions. In all, Edison owned 1,093 patents in his lifetime. He defined his inventiveness as "1 percent genius and 99 percent perspiration."

Edison experimented in many fields. He tried to invent things that worked under normal conditions with few parts and were easy to repair. Edison also improved others' inventions, including the typewriter, the motion picture camera, and the electric generator. He was credited with almost inventing the radio and predicting the harnessing of atomic energy.

Edison had a reputation for working continuously for days at a time, stopping only for short naps. He was never frustrated by failure. Rather, he said he had just found one other way something didn't work.

It seemed wherever Thomas Edison worked, he invented or improved existing inventions. For example, in 1863, Edison became a telegrapher in Boston, where, in 1869, he perfected an electric vote-recording machine. In that latter year, he moved to New York. Penniless, he convinced a friend who was an employee of the Fold Indicator Company to let him sleep in the office. Here, Edison studied the stock ticker. Before long, he was earning $300 a month fixing the machines. Along the way, he made improvements. The president of the Gold and Stock Telegraph Company offered to purchase the rights to the changes Edison had made. Thinking the improvements were worth $4,000 or $5,000, Edison was shocked to be offered $40,000 when he suggested, "Well, General, suppose you make me an offer."

In 1876, when he was twenty-nine years old, Edison opened a workshop in Menlo Park, New Jersey. Here, in 1877, he improved the typewriter and invented the phonograph. Throughout his life, Edison said this was his favorite invention. Although he was plagued with a partial hearing loss, Edison listened to the phonograph by placing his head close to it and listening to the music's vibrations.

Inventions poured out of him. In 1879, he worked out the principle for the electric light bulb and immediately set a goal to bring electric lights to every household. Using a filament of carbonized thread inside a bulb, Edison created a light that burned for twenty-four hours. By 1914, he had connected the phonograph and camera to make talking pictures. He also invented the duplicating machine, the cement mixer, and the dictaphone.

Edison married Mary Stilwell in 1871 and fathered three children. Stilwell died in 1884, and Edison remarried in 1886, fathering three more children. It is doubtful either marriage was happy. The independent inventor loved his work and spent most of his time in his workshops, setting aside only July 4 of each year to celebrate with his family.

As he aged, Edison became fascinated with life after death. He told reporters that he was working on something "so sensitive that if there is life after death, it will pick up the evidence of it." But after Edison's death, on October 18, 1931, no such device was ever found.

tion double, so that by 1907, two hundred and fifty thousand people lived in the Hollywood area.

In 1904, Hollywood's City Attorney Young claimed, "Hollywood can never be a large business center, but it is being more and more recognized as a city of homes." Soon, however, Hollywood would become the center for one of the country's newest industries, the motion picture industry. The first studio in Hollywood, owned by the Nestor Company, was opened in 1911, and the first full-scale Hollywood movie, Cecil B. De Mille's *The Squaw Man*, was released in 1914.

Camera Magic

In 1902, Georges Melies accidentally discovered trick photography while filming a street scene of a carriage in Paris. The camera jammed and it took a few minutes to correct it before filming restarted. While the crew worked to unjam the film, the carriage passed by. As filming recommenced, a hearse rolled down the street. When the film was processed, Melies discovered that the carriage he had originally been filming when the camera jammed looked as though it had magically turned into the hearse. Inspired by his discovery, Melies then built the first European film studio, where he worked to perfect many exciting new special effects.

The pictures that patrons viewed on the large screen were jumpy and overexposed because they were photographed in bright daylight. They were also silent, using printed subtitles to replace dialogue. Many theaters accompanied their short films with tunes played onstage by the local organist. American arcade owners had to purchase rather than rent their films. Then the first film exchange was opened by a cameraman, Harry H. Miles, and movie programs could be changed twice a week.

Film Tales

Perhaps the single greatest advance in early movie making was in the creation in 1903 of *The Great Train Robbery*. This eleven-minute motion picture, directed by Edwin S. Porter, was the first movie to have a plot. While telling the story of a bank

Nickelodeons, shown in this 1907 painting by John Sloan, provided cheap entertainment and were very popular with the poor immigrant populations in big cities. Movies could be purchased cheaply or rented from film exchanges, and old shops and storerooms could be converted to theaters simply by adding rows of chairs and a piano; nickelodeons sprang up by the thousands across the country.

The Great Train Robbery, *made in 1903, excited audiences with new dramatic effects. Here, in a chase scene, robbers are shown gaining on a train. Throughout the decade producers concentrated on extending the dramatic possibilities of moving film.*

robbery and the subsequent capture of the thieves, Porter edited scenes of robbers escaping and mixed them with scenes of a posse in hot pursuit to create a feeling of suspense. This was also the first motion picture to be shot out of sequence, because Porter realized that to tell the story, he would need to cut back and forth between varied settings. He filmed the scenes from each setting one at a time, then wove them into each other to fit his story. Prints of the film were hand colored and included a dramatic close-up of an outlaw taking aim and firing at the camera. Projectionists were advised to open or close the film with this scene. Excited theatergoers insisted that the scene be shown over and over again.

The St. Louis World's Fair hosted *Hales Tours and Scenes of the World.* This filmed sequence of the country's landmarks was shown to audiences sitting in simulated railroad carriages. In 1905, a movie theater designed solely to show short movies was built in Pittsburgh, Pennsylvania. Called nickelodeons because the cost of admission was five cents, the theaters proved popular and sprouted across the country. By 1908, there were eight to ten thousand nickelodeons in the nation.

By the middle of the decade, special effects had been tried by many of the country's producers. In 1907, Edwin S. Porter produced *Rescued from an Eagle's Nest*, a film that depicted a child being carried off by an eagle. The child star of this film was D. W. Griffith, who would later become a great director himself. Using special effects, *Ben Hur* and *The*

Count of Monte Cristo were filmed for the first time the same year.

The lead actors in all these films were not credited. It was not uncommon for movie actors and actresses to remain anonymous. Movie acting at that time was considered degrading compared to live acting in the theater. But the very fact that the motion picture was bigger than life made it difficult to thwart the development of stars. The public soon picked out their favorite actors and actresses and held them up for adulation. In 1909, the silent heroine Mary Pickford made her debut and very soon became America's sweetheart.

Popular Songs and Pluggers

While some tunes were simply written as background accompaniment for the movies, most popular music was written for singing. At home, groups gathered around the family piano and sang sentimental and happy songs.

Sheet music was sold at almost every cheap store. Song pluggers, who had been hired by music publishers, traveled the country to play the new music in public so that the tunes would gain an audience. They visited dime stores and restaurants, and cajoled orchestra leaders into playing their music. They packed their pianos on to horse-drawn carts and often performed for gathering crowds along the way. With the advent of cinemas, the song pluggers used the theaters to demonstrate their new music. They encouraged theater owners to flash a series of lantern slides with the song lyrics on the screen during movie breaks, while the song pluggers played

the music and audiences sang along.

More than a hundred popular songs sold over a million copies every year for the first ten years of the century. Two of the most popular songs were "School Days" and "Sweet Adeline." The latter became the hallmark of groups of men who gathered at corner barbershops to harmonize. "In the Good Old Summertime" also drew record sales during this decade.

Hot Tunes and High Culture

Ragtime probably caught on because it gave audiences an alternative to these sentimental ballads and to waltzes, which were still popular at the time. Ragtime melodies were catchy because of the syncopation or surprising accents placed on weak beats played over a regular bass rhythm. The music originated as instrumental banjo and piano music along the Mississippi River shortly after the Civil War. It traveled along the Mississippi as riverfront dance halls caught the excitement of these catchy tunes.

By the 1900s, Scott Joplin, a black musician from Texarkana, Arkansas, who had studied classical music, had written and published scores for such ragtime hits as "Maple Leaf Rag," "Under the Bamboo Tree," and "Hello Ma Baby." Soon brass bands were playing these scores. Joplin's contemporaries, including Irving Berlin, were drawn to his music and began to create additional scores as ragtime quickly became part of mainstream dance music.

Countering the upbeat mood of ragtime was the serious tone of the blues. This music probably originated in the sun-baked fields of southern plantations when black laborers sang out their worries and frustrations. The blues relied on flat notes to create a moody, wailing tone. At first, the songs were accompanied by hand clapping and foot stomping or home-made instruments like washboards and pots and pans. Later, banjos and guitars, then pianos, and finally whole bands of instrumentalists performed the music. Sometimes the blues contained strange harmonies and breaks during which people shouted "Oh Lawdy" or "Oh Baby!" These would become known in the later world of jazz as riffs, in which musicians would add variations and otherwise embroider the music.

While the phonograph was still a novelty, many cities had their own orchestras. European companies toured the United States with productions of operas such as Richard Strauss's *Elektra*, which caused controversy because it contained violence, and Giacomo Puccini's *Madame Butterfly*. In late 1903, Richard Wagner's *Parsifal* was also produced at the Metropolitan. Four years later, Richard Strauss's *Salome*, with its seductive dance scene, was presented at the Metropolitan Opera House, but New York audiences proved a conservative lot and it was quickly withdrawn.

Entertainment-hungry Audiences

When the orchestra had a night off, vaudeville shows were the place to be. Here new musicians could be heard. As urban populations continued to grow, the size of audiences hungry for entertainment also increased.

Theater owners were no doubt thrilled with their packed houses when vaudeville troops came to town.

It probably never occurred to most people that the theaters in

which they were entertained were potential firetraps. It would take a tragedy to make them aware of their dangers. On December 30, 1903, the Iroquois Theater in Chicago burned to the ground, killing 588 people. The theater orchestra kept playing to the packed audience until the smoke became too much for the musicians.

Richard Strauss's opera Salome *was denounced as immoral by New York audiences and withdrawn from performance after a few days in 1907. It contains a dance in which Salome takes off seven veils.*

At one point, Eddie Foy, the principal comedian, ran onstage and dropped his son into the orchestra pit, hoping that members of the orchestra would bring the boy to safety. Once the fire was extinguished, firefighters discovered bodies stacked seven feet high at the fire exits. The tragedy led to new theater codes in almost every American city, requiring fire walls, more exits with doors opening outward, fire proofing, and unobstructed alleyways.

Vaudeville's popularity was undiminished. On April 25, 1904, Will Rogers made his debut as an entertainer at Madison Square Garden, in New York City, regaling audiences with his rope tricks and homespun humor. He began his career as a cowboy but found fame on stage, chewing gum and performing tricks while making wry comments on the changing life, times, and attitudes of Americans. The comic philosopher,

who was one-eighth Cherokee, kidded about the government, people, and politics. His catch phrases, "All I know is what I read in the papers," and, "I never met a man I didn't like," echoed throughout the land.

Baseball Booms

Another popular entertainment for Americans was sport, especially baseball. The National League had existed since 1876, and in 1900, the Western League became the American League. With two distinct leagues, it was only fitting that play-offs be held. The first World Series was played in 1903, between Boston of the American League and Pittsburgh of the National League. At the Huntington Avenue Ball Field in Boston, the home side captured the series, winning by five games to three.

Some famous names from this era included Connie Mack, who became the manager of the Philadelphia Athletics in 1901; John J. McGraw, or "Little Napoleon," became the manager of the New York Giants in 1902. In an American League game on May 9, 1904, Cy Young, a pitcher for the Boston team, shut out Philadelphia without allowing a man to reach first base, a feat achieved only twice before in baseball's short history. After pitching three shutouts in the 1905 World Series, Christy Mathewson was considered the Giants' greatest pitcher.

But the best all-around player during this decade had to be Ty Cobb, who played for Detroit. Cobb could play and hit better and more consistently than any other player in the history of baseball, winning

Will Rogers was an entertainer who mixed rope tricks with humorous comments on American life. As a young man he traveled the world, and afterwards used his skills as a ranch hand and cow-puncher in his stage act. He appears in full cowboy regalia here at his first vaudeville show in New York City in 1904. Later he appeared in movies, wrote many books, and made frequent radio broadcasts. He became a folk hero, offering homespun philosophy and commentary on the news of the day.

Ty Cobb. (1886-1961)

This proud, hypersensitive, and intelligent man proved to be the all-time leading hitter in the major leagues, with a .367 batting average, totalling 4,191 hits and 2,244 runs in his career. He won twelve American League batting titles, nine of them in consecutive years from 1907 to 1915. Cobb stole a career total of 829 bases.

Despite his accomplishments, Cobb was probably one of the most unpopular players in baseball history. He played with the Detroit Tigers from 1905 until 1926, and was remembered as a man who handled teasing poorly, was quick to lose his temper, and was unable to accept even the smallest failures. While on the road, he often ate alone and spent his spare time wandering museums and libraries or practicing to be a better ballplayer.

Tyrus Cobb, one of three children, was born in Narrows, Banks County, Georgia. His father, a professor and the mayor of Royston, pushed his children to get as much education as possible and hoped that Tyrus would grow up to be a lawyer or physician. Cobb never got over the feeling that he had disappointed his father by becoming a ballplayer. But his only dream was to play ball. At one point, the young boy tried to trade some of his father's books for a baseball glove. Even as a child, his obsession with winning affected Cobb's playing. He recalled, "I . . . saw no point in losing, if I could win!"

As a child, Cobb spent his summer and winter vacations at his grandparents' house, where he played in pickup ball games. At home in Royston, he played with a young boys' team, called the Rompers. By the age of fourteen, he had been recruited by the city's club team, the Royston Reds. The left-handed hitter and right-handed thrower was showered with coins from the fans after winning city games. The $10 or $11 Cobb picked up was the first income he had ever earned playing ball. "Once an athlete feels the peculiar thrill that goes with victory and the public praise, he's bewitched," declared Cobb. "He can never get away from it."

During the winter of 1904, Cobb wrote to the South Atlantic League requesting a tryout. He was told to report at his own expense to the Augusta Tourists. When Cobb told his father that he planned to pursue a career in the league, his father responded, "Don't come home a failure."

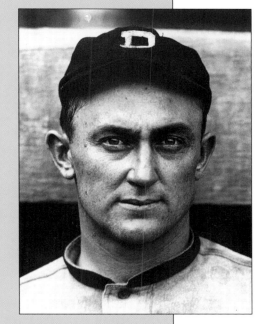

By the end of July 1905, Cobb had made over one hundred hits and was being scouted by big league teams, but Cobb's father would never share in his son's success. On August 9, 1905, Cobb learned his father had been shot and killed by Cobb's mother when she discovered he had been having an affair. Ten days later, at the age of eighteen, Cobb was notified that he had been purchased by the Detroit Tigers. Within a year, sportswriters were calling the talented young man "The Georgia Peach" and promising "he will be a good hummer," and that he would become "a sensational fielder and thrower."

Cobb lived out his promise. On Sunday, September 29, 1907, he helped his team to a pennant victory, becoming the youngest man ever to win a big league batting championship, with 212 hits for the year and a batting average of .350. The Tigers were defeated in that series by the Chicago Cubs, but 1908 and 1909 brought two more pennants for the young man. Despite his successes on the baseball diamond, Cobb's mood swings made him a difficult man to befriend. When he died in 1961, not a single fellow ballplayer attended his funeral.

twelve American League batting titles. Nicknamed "The Georgia Peach," he was also known as a fierce competitor, unpopular for his rough play.

The games and players were followed religiously by small boys, who spent their idle time playing sandlot ball, and by men and women who attended games or followed the

Albert Goodwill Spalding. (1850-1915)

A. G. Spalding, the cofounder of baseball's National League, was professional baseball's first superstar and manager and owner of the Chicago White Stockings.

Brought up in Byron, Illinois, Spalding learned early to promote himself and his interests in order to prosper. After the death of his father in 1858, Spalding's mother sent him to board with an aunt in Rockford. As a twelve-year-old, Spalding remembered being lonesome and homesick. He recalled that going to the commons and watching other boys play ball provided "the only bright skies for me in those dark days of utter loneliness."

In 1865, he joined the Rockford Forest City club as their pitcher. At the time, baseball was a recreational amusement for upper-class urban gentlemen. The club rules stated that no one could receive pay for playing, and expenses were covered by membership dues rather than paid admission. Between 1867 and 1870, Spalding led the club to forty-five victories in fifty-eight games.

In 1870, the club went on a seventeen-game eastern tour, winning thirteen games, tying one, and losing three. After the tour, Spalding decided to make baseball, which by then was growing into a professional sport, his career.

On July 24, 1875, he joined the Chicago White Stockings, and in 1876, he cofounded the National Baseball League with the aid of William Hulbert. The men planned to reduce the game to a manageable business system by increasing competition, making it stable, popularizing it, and eliminating the gambling and betting that seemed to surround the sport. Though Spalding actually played a secondary role in establishing the National League, he would take complete credit for this in his later years. In 1876, Spalding founded the sporting goods company that still carries his name.

Spalding lived by the motto "everything is possible to him who dares." His reputation as the country's best pitcher enhanced his sales success while helping to establish the game's popularity. On April 18, 1891, Spalding retired from baseball.

In 1906 while talking to schoolchildren in Manhattan, Spalding said, "We live in a strenuous age, and our American boys and youth should be educated and developed along the lines that will enable them to meet and cope with these conditions." Athletics, he concluded, especially baseball, was the best method to ready them "for the rough and tumble business life of today."

Spalding promoted the sport to serve his own sporting interest but also to solidify the game's place in American hearts. He also once told the chairman of the National Baseball Commission, "With a little encouragement, aid and cooperation from those prominently connected with the game in the United States, I am confident that the time will come when baseball will become the established and recognized field sport in the world."

results in the nation's newspapers.

Perhaps the greatest boon to American baseball was A. G. Spalding, the cofounder, along with William Hulbert, of the National Baseball League, in 1876. Spalding, who was considered one of the sport's first superstar pitchers, played for, was president of, and managed the Chicago White Stockings during the late 1800s. Hoping to professionalize baseball by reducing the game to a manageable business system, he planned to increase competition and make it stable and more widely popular.

Spalding also founded a sports equipment company, which still bears his name, and his reputation as baseball's best pitcher greatly enhanced his sales success.

Sports in Their Infancy

Boxing was a less respectable sport. In fact it was illegal in some areas, but it was still popular. Boxing did not really come of age until 1920, when New York passed the Walker Law, making it legal to prize-fight publicly. James J. Jeffries held the heavyweight boxing title from 1899 until 1905. Jack Johnson became the first African-American champion in 1908, when he defeated Tommy Burns in Australia.

There was no pro-football at that time. The game was mostly played on college and university campuses across the country and was followed by many college graduates. The sport was gaining in popularity during this time, however, and in 1905, fifty parlor cars were hired to take society's elite to New Haven to see Yale play Princeton.

Newspaper and Magazine Innovations

When sports fans were not attending the games, they liked to read about them in the papers. Changes in printing technology greatly improved magazine and newspaper production during this part of the century. Photographic techniques such as the halftone process and photolithography were developed,

In 1908, Jack Johnson became the first African-American to take the world heavyweight boxing title, but his win provoked violent racial prejudice. Boxing at this time was not a respectable sport and was even illegal in some areas.

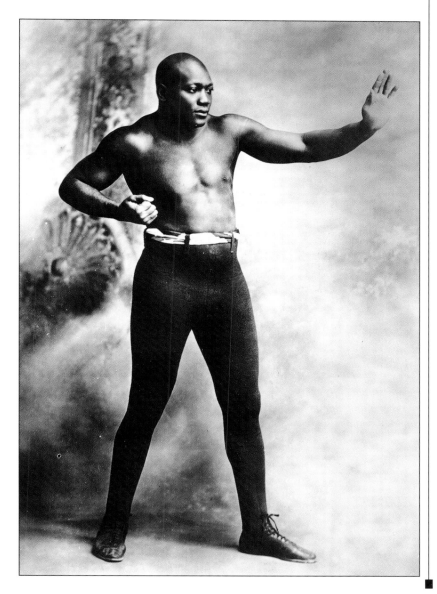

Football was a college game that was growing in popularity. It was an incredibly dangerous sport, however, in which many died, and in 1906 and 1910, rules were changed to reduce the numbers of fatalities and crippling injuries. Frank Merriwell was an important figure in popular literature in 1900.

enabling newspapers and magazines to be more profusely illustrated. In 1905, Ira Rubell, an American papermaker, accidentally transferred ink images on to the rubber cylinder of his rotary press instead of onto paper, thereby inventing offset printing.

With the advent of new public

A selection of magazines available to the literate New Yorker in 1900. Printing technology was improving, and magazines strove to become more attractive and cheaper to compete with each other. Scare stories, sensational headlines, and cartoons were introduced to attract readers.

relations techniques, reporters for newspapers and magazines gained access to information on business events. For example, in 1906, Ivy Lee was hired as public relations counsel for the Pennsylvania Railroad. Following an accident near Gap, Pennsylvania, Lee insisted on "absolute frankness" and invited reporters to the scene at the railroad's expense, setting a precedent for reporters' access to this kind of news. Lee, who had graduated from Princeton and worked as a reporter for the New York *Journal*, the *Times* and the *World*, established the public relations firm of Parker and Lee with the motto "Accuracy, Authenticity, Interest." Lee never tried to deceive the press but sent releases to newspapers with the statement that it was "written on behalf of the client and that no money would be paid for its insertion in the columns of any newspaper."

Shortly after Lee handled the Pennsylvania Railroad incident, an accident occurred on the New York Central Railroad. Reporters were kept away and the details were hushed up. In response, reporters gave the New York Central bad press. Soon railroads followed Lee's policy of working openly with the press. This signalled a new awareness that businesses and government needed to cater to a vast consumer public made more knowledgeable by access to news and information.

Newspaper Wars

Two newspaper magnates, William Randolph Hearst and Joseph Pulitzer, turned producing newspapers into a war when, to boost circulation, they began adding special sections including sports, cartoons, and features. The publishers created

Newspaper cartoons were very popular, and in 1907, the San Francisco Chronicle *decided to try to boost circulation by printing "Mutt and Jeff," a comic strip adventure created by H. C. "Bud" Fisher, six days a week.*

"scare headlines" in huge type that made threatening statements or ominous predictions, and hired columnists to write sensational columns and stories to attract customers. The stories in the Hearst and Pulitzer newspapers were soon labelled "Yellow Journalism," originally because they both carried the popular comic strip, "The Yellow Kid." Eventually, the term came to refer to the scare tactics and sensational styles of the newspapers.

Newspaper cartoons had been around before 1900, but during this decade they went from single frame cartoons to strips. The most popular characters were "Happy Hooligan," "The Katzenjammer Kids," and "Buster Brown." In 1907, the *San Francisco Chronicle* added "Mutt and Jeff" to the cartoon page, which was now nicknamed the "funnies."

Magazines Promote Social Change

Some popular and widely read magazines were *Nation*, *McClure's*, which was the most popular forum for the muckrakers, and *Outlook*, which serialized *Up from Slavery* by Booker T. Washington. A news magazine, *World's Work,* made its appearance in 1900, concerning itself with the "activities of the newly organized world, its problems and even its romances." In 1909, the *Progressive* was published for the first time by followers of the progressive Wisconsin Senate leader Robert M. La Follette. The *Progressive* published articles written with a Socialist and working Americans' reformer perspective.

From the funnies to baseball to silent movies, Americans romanticized the changes in their country and tried to avoid the darker side of life. But some Americans would take this as a challenge. They intended to make America answerable for all its social and political problems.

Coney Island in the early 1900s was a popular place of amusement and relaxation for the citizens of New York. This picture shows the "helter skelter" in Luna Park.

CHAPTER 4
Roosevelt and the Progressives

Colonel Theodore Roosevelt leads the Rough Riders in a charge up San Juan Hill (also known as Kettle Hill), Cuba, in the Spanish-American War of 1898. Brave and bold as a soldier, his energy and charisma got him elected governor of New York in the same year.

He wanted to be president of the United States, but Theodore J. Roosevelt hated the idea of sitting in the vice president's office. He believed beyond question that it was a do-nothing job and a political dead end. In fact, Roosevelt only became vice president because Republican party bosses wanted him out of their way. They pressured the young New York governor into joining the incumbent President McKinley on the 1900 Republican ticket after Vice President Garret Hobart died in 1899.

In the early part of this century, there were no direct primary elec-tions to nominate public officials. Instead, people voted only to elect representatives, called delegates, to choose public officials. The delegates themselves were controlled by party bosses, who often had also selected them as candidates for their offices. In some cases, the bosses even paid vot-ers to vote for the delegates. In turn, these delegates frequently handpicked only those candidates who would toe the party line. Today, such indirect primaries are illegal because, early this century, they had put govern-ment control into the hands of a few powerful people.

Party bosses had become wary of Roosevelt when, as the newly appointed New York Police Commissioner, the popular Roosevelt had proven to be an independent leader who said what was on his mind. As early as 1895, Roosevelt had taken up the gauntlet with the Republican party managers by speaking out against the alliances formed between big business, criminals, and politicians. A man with progressive ideas for his time, Roosevelt aligned himself firmly with the New York community against political corruption.

". . . this Madman and the Presidency. . . ."

Roosevelt had been elected governor of New York because party bosses recognized the man's charisma. It was a charisma developed through determination and drive. Even as a young child, Theodore Roosevelt had been able to overcome asthma simply by determination and living what he called "the strenuous life," a life that constantly pitted his physical strength against nature. The son of wealthy New Yorkers, he was educated for a life of public service at Harvard University. Upon graduating, he spent two years on a ranch in North Dakota building his health. He enjoyed challenging friends and, later, cabinet members, to races and hikes in order to show off his own agility and stamina. As a colonel of the U.S. Army Volunteers, he was a hero of the Spanish-American War. Known to be brave, brash, and bold almost to the point of foolishness, he often bragged of his prowess as one

of the Rough Riders, a U.S. Army cavalry group.

As a politician, he was a fine orator, able to hold an audience in the palm of his hand while he spoke. His charismatic personality enabled him to push civil service reform and tax bills through the New York State Legislature. Often these were bills opposed by the party bosses.

Consequently, the Republican bigwigs who controlled the party jumped at the opportunity to place Roosevelt in a role they believed would limit his reforms. Only one Republican leader, Mark Hanna, saw the enormous power Roosevelt could obtain. The conservative leader with tight ties to big business implored his fellow Republicans to reconsider. He asked, "Don't any of you realize that there's only one life between this madman and the presidency?" He could not have known how prophetic his question was.

Upon accepting the nomination, Roosevelt was told he would be expected to do the majority of campaign speechmaking and traveling as President McKinley would only hold his customary front porch receptions for visiting dignitaries. Roosevelt agreed cheerfully. "I'm as strong as a bull moose and you can use me to the limit."

Death Plays a Hand

With Roosevelt as his running mate, McKinley was reelected on November 7, 1900. Roosevelt took valiantly to the vice presidency. He moved to Washington, D.C., and began to play out his role. But fate turned the tables on Roosevelt when, on September 6, 1901, McLeon

"The other day the most famous gambler in New York, long known as one of the most prominent criminals in this city, was reported as saying that by February everything would again 'be running wide open;' in other words, that the gambler, the disorderly housekeeper, and the lawbreaking liquor-seller would be plying their trades once more. . . . Undoubtedly there are many politicians who are bent on seeing this. . . The politician who wishes to use the police department for his own base purposes, and the criminal and the trafficker in vice . . . are quite right in using every effort to drive us out of office. It is for you decent people to say whether or not they shall succeed."

Roosevelt, in a speech to the Methodist Ministers' Association.

Czolgosz, an anarchist, walked up to McKinley at the Temple of Music in Buffalo, New York, as if to shake his hand. Then he shot the president in the chest and abdomen. Although McKinley rallied for a few days and appeared to be recovering, he died of his wounds eight days later, on September 14, 1901.

While McKinley's condition was worsening, an intensive search began for the vice president, who was on a hiking trip in the Adirondack Mountains. After he was located on top of Mount Marcy, he rushed by horse and fast car to a nearby village and then sped by special train to Buffalo. At 2:30 P.M., on September 14, in a borrowed high hat that was the wrong size, Roosevelt took the oath of office to become the twenty-sixth and then youngest president of the United States. He would also become one of the most popular presidents in history.

Wisely avoiding conflict with party leaders, he promised to continue McKinley's path and keep his appointments "for the peace, the prosperity, and the honor of our beloved country." He promised radical change, yet nevertheless chose to obtain the support of the public and conservative party leaders before he turned the country's path toward reform.

On December 3, 1901, Roosevelt gave his first annual message to Congress. On the surface, he supported the Old Guard, or the conservative political and big business leaders who had been responsible for helping him achieve political success. But he also indicated there must be some regulation of trusts or monopolies. He was not against big business per se, but he did attack what he called bad business and business owners who sought to control the government.

Big Business Has a Hand in Government

Since the Civil War, business influences had dominated government to such an extent that big business practically ran the government. McKinley's office had been no exception. Republican party boss, Mark Hanna, had kept the federal government quarantined from crusading reformers and their proposals. Typical of bosses of this time, Hanna had obtained campaign gifts from corporations and wealthy individuals. In return the federal government was expected to repay contributions with legislation that protected the contributors.

The bosses were known as the "invisible government." Hanna himself had so much power that he had usually been able to manipulate nominations so that only "safe" men became candidates for office. The best of these candidates would vote only for those bills the party bosses wanted to get passed.

An "old boys" system had developed, consisting of business leaders and the politicians who promoted legislation to help both remain in power. It was firmly in place by the time Roosevelt came into office. So strong was the party leader's power that a "senatorial courtesy" existed. Even presidential appointments to individual states were only approved if the senator from the state agreed. The bosses also ran national conventions, where politicians controlling large blocs of votes could influence this system and even the selection of a

Mark Hanna. (1837-1904)

Mark Hanna, a Cleveland, Ohio, industrialist, emerged as the chairman of the Republican National Committee during the late 1800s and remained a powerful political figure until his death in 1904. As chairman, Hanna had the power to choose Republican candidates and determine their policies.

Hanna supported Wall Street in theory and practice, and as party boss, he was responsible for persuading large business leaders to contribute to the Republican Party. In exchange, he encouraged Republicans in office to legislate in favor of those businesses. At the same time, he wanted to help laborers as well as capitalists.

Hanna was responsible for helping his friend William McKinley to win the presidential election in 1896 and was helpful to Theodore Roosevelt's campaign for governor of New York the same year. After McKinley's election, Hanna's influence grew to enormous proportions, and in 1897, he was elected a U.S. senator from Ohio.

Despite his dislike of Theodore Roosevelt, Hanna helped Roosevelt end the anthracite coal miners' strike in 1902 by persuading mine owners to reach a settlement with the workers. Hanna, who had made his early fortune in groceries, coal, and iron before he entered politics, believed that industry should accept unions because they were easier to deal with than unorganized but dissatisfied workers. He reasoned that better wages and working conditions would lessen the chances of class warfare and eliminate the push among the working class toward socialism or communism.

Hanna was said to be a man of sincerity of purpose, of great courage and loyalty, and unswerving devotion to the interests of the nation and the people. After McKinley's death, when Roosevelt had been sworn in as president, Hanna called on him and promised his loyalty. Taking Roosevelt's outstretched hand, he offered, "Mr. President, I wish you success and a prosperous administration. I trust you will command me if I can be of any service."

presidential candidate. Businesses unhappy with a party boss's choice of candidates could withhold contributions from the boss.

Under this system, proposals for regulating rates or wages, for fixing maximum hours for workers, for compulsory arbitration of labor disputes, or for legislation otherwise detrimental to big business, were viewed as interference with the economy. Protective tariffs, land grants, franchises, and all legislation that benefited industry, however, were acceptable areas for politicians to make laws in, according to big business. Business leaders supported these ideas by referring to a convenient, popularly-accepted theory called Social Darwinism.

Social Darwinism became popular in the late nineteenth century. Despite its obvious contradiction of humane and Christian principles, it continued to influence society in the early twentieth century. The theory was first developed by Charles Darwin, through studies charting survival of the fittest in the animal kingdom. It was then suggested by Herbert Spencer, an English political philosopher, that the theory could also apply to the human race. Spencer believed that in the human struggle, destruction of the weak and survival of the fit were essential to human progress. The strong survived because they were innately superior. Any government efforts to help the weak survive were futile and dangerous because these efforts would weaken society's progress toward greatness.

Social Darwinism was promoted in America by William Graham Sumner, an historian and professor at Yale. His followers included many famous industrialists, among them Andrew Carnegie. The influence of Social Darwinism diminished after Sumner's death in 1910 and with the growing popularity of a number of political movements that began in the 1890s and 1900s. These movements, which included Populism and Progressivism, argued against the prevailing big business control of and attitude toward laborers and the government.

Populists and Progressives

The Populist Party was formed in 1892 as an alliance of farmers from all over the country. Since the railroad monopolies charged such high prices for transporting agricultural goods, the Populists demanded that the government assume ownership of the railroads. And since they were forced to go to the banks for loans to pay for farmland and machinery at a time when they received less money for their crops, the Populists also argued for the govern-

ment to issue more money. Instead of having big business control the government, they wanted to change the voting system to more accurately reflect voters' desires. This they would achieve by having senators elected by a direct vote, by initiating a secret ballot, and by controlling government spending by allowing citizens to vote on specific referendums. They also wanted to restrict immigration, institute a graduated income tax, and to conserve the national domain — federally owned land, waterways, and mountain areas, some rich in mineral deposits.

While the Populist movement began in the countryside, the Progressives were primarily city based. Though they praised the efficient techniques of big business, they were concerned about the effects of Social Darwinism and thought a well-run government could and should protect the public interest and the common laborer. Many Progressives believed that the government should help improve housing and the social environment, ensure high quality in food, regulate or outlaw child labor, and, like the Populists, end the control over the government held by railroads and other powerful special interests and industries.

Although the Progressive movement was led by Wisconsin Senator Robert Marion La Follette, by 1912, Roosevelt would be nominated as the Progressive presidential candidate. The party would bear the nickname the "Bull Moose party," after Roosevelt.

Roosevelt on the Fence

Socialists also had a political voice at this time, represented by their leader, Eugene V. Debs, who sup-

"If we do not like the survival of the fittest, we have only one possible alternative, and that is survival of the unfittest."

William G. Sumner

Robert Marion La Follette, Sr. (1855-1925)

Robert La Follette, Sr. was born in a two-room log cabin, a sketch of which he always used on his campaign literature. He was sometimes called "Battling Bob" because of his reformist politics that went against the grain of party politics of the era. Even as a student at the University of Wisconsin, in Madison, La Follette demonstrated his insurgent tendencies when he attempted to reorganize some student groups.

La Follette became a lawyer in 1880 and was elected a U.S. representative in 1885. In 1890, La Follette returned to Wisconsin to practice law.

La Follette already had a history of working poorly with people when elected governor of Wisconsin in 1900. Still, his tactics worked to bulldoze several reforms. The progressive governor led Wisconsin into becoming one of the first states to enact a direct primary in which senators were elected by popular vote rather than through delegate nominations. While La Follette was governor, the state legislature also agreed to sweeping conservation measures and government control of railroad rates. Through legislation, the property taxes of corporations were also brought into line with taxes on all other Wisconsin properties. Until then, corporations had been paying less taxes per acre of property than others.

From 1906 to 1925, La Follette was a U.S. senator and advocated strict railroad regulations, lower tariffs, conservation, and better conditions for American sailors. Later in his term, the senator opposed entry into World War I and United States membership in the League of Nations. La Follette was considered a dramatic, heroic crusader against wrong. He worked for the good of the common person, though his inability to work well with others made him at times a hindrance to his party.

After Taft's election, La Follette admitted he was disillusioned with the Republican party. He said, "From this time on I am going to be independent. I am going to serve my conscience. I have been lecturing, I have saved my dollars and put them into a farm up there in Iowa. . . ."

La Follette didn't retire to Iowa, and he continued to influence politics. In January 1909, he began publishing the *La Follette's Weekly Magazine*, which would later be called the *Progressive*. In his first issue, he proclaimed, "Open-eyed at last we are startled to find our great industrial organizations in control of politics, government and national resources. They manage conventions, make platforms, dictate legislation. They rule through the very men elected to represent the people."

ported labor reform. The Socialists believed the government should intervene in American economic life to promote social justice. Socialist goals would establish a cooperative commonwealth. Under this system, the government would own businesses, create relief for the unemployed, shorten the work week, and abolish child labor. Socialists, too, wanted voting reform and pressed for equal suffrage, referendums, and proportional representation. Their program included a number of reforms that were to be initiated by Congress — reforms such as social security laws, income and inheritance taxes, and the abolition of the Supreme Court's power to pass upon the constitutionality of legislation.

Although Roosevelt believed in some Socialist reforms such as child labor laws and civil rights legislation for minorities and women, he was perceptive enough to realize that he couldn't challenge party politics to make these things happen. He often played both sides of the fence, promoting himself as a man of the people while attempting to soothe the industrialists who had the ear of powerful Republicans.

New Yorkers had to stand in line for coal during the 1902 coal strike. Coal was the main heating fuel of the time, and people feared a shortage as the winter approached.

Labor Rights

At the same time, Roosevelt was one of the first presidents to act on behalf of labor. He would interfere in business, and he was not afraid to stand up when he saw workers being exploited. For example, in 1902, Roosevelt responded to a coal strike by encouraging mine owners and union representatives to accept arbitration by an outside party. The strike, which was paralyzing many parts of the country, immediately affected mines in Ohio, Illinois, West Virginia, and Pennsylvania — all mines owned by the railroads.

Miners worked long hours for low pay. They lived in company-owned housing and could only buy goods from higher priced stores owned by the companies. In order to obtain better pay and conditions, the miners had joined the United Mine Workers, led by John Mitchell.

In 1902, the miners demanded a 20 percent wage increase, an eight-hour day, improved working conditions, and union recognition. The mine owners, headed by George F. Baer, president of Reading Railroad, refused to budge and set out to break the unions. Baer declared, "The rights and interests of the laboring man will be protected and cared for — not by the labor agitators, but by the Christian men to whom God in his wisdom has given control of the property interests of this country." In the summer of that year, the miners struck.

By mid-September, the union and mine operators had made no progress. Roosevelt refused to side with either the coal mine owners or the laborers. He intervened by appointing an arbitration commission composed of mine owners and one former union official, whom he called a sociologist, to settle differences fairly. It spent four months questioning more than five hundred witnesses to determine the needs of operators and miners. In a decision handed down in March 1903, the miners were awarded partial settlement of their demands. They received a 10 percent wage increase, an eight-hour day for engineers, firemen and pumpmen, and the right to submit future grievances to a board of conciliation — gains that were not as great as the unions had hoped. In fact, their main goal, to have mine owners recognize the union, was not achieved.

Roosevelt claimed he had done his duty, which was to steer a middle course and bring about a peaceful

William "Big Bill" Dudley Haywood. (1869-1928)

When he was three years old, following his father's death, William Dudley Haywood's mother took him to Ophir, a rough, tough mining town. Here, Haywood learned to fight hard and mean to get what he wanted. Growing up, he witnessed street brawls and duels and became street smart. His formal schooling ended by the time he was ten.

He went to work on a local farm for room, board, and one dollar a month. At fifteen, Haywood went to Nevada where he wheeled loads of rock from the mines. He found the work hard and unrewarding, but as a miner, he heard stories about the Haymarket riots in Chicago and the Coeur d'Alene, Idaho strike, where angry miners had dynamited the company's mill. He listened eagerly to the stories and formed his own ideas about the downtrodden. He learned how force and violence could win strikes. As he learned, Haywood became convinced that the American way of dealing with the working class was wrong. He believed that the laborer should, rather than earn a small wage for hard work, share in all company profits, and that the workers should take over industry.

In 1905, Haywood helped to organize and became president of the Industrial Workers of the World (IWW) to try and achieve these ideals. This radical organization was composed of untrained and unskilled laborers.

Samuel Gompers, president of the American Federation of Labor, refused to have anything to do with Haywood or his organization. Gompers found Haywood's tactics, which included sabotage and violence, so offensive that he forbade his members from joining the IWW. Consequently, the IWW was filled with malcontents who often refused work when it was offered.

In 1905, Haywood was jailed for one year to await trial for the murder of Idaho's ex-governor Frank Steunenberg, who was killed by a bomb in his home. It was Steunenberg who, six years earlier, had brutally suppressed the Coeur d'Arlene strike. Evidence against Haywood consisted of one man's testimony. Harry Orchard said he had been paid $300 by Haywood to kill the ex-governor.

At his trial, Haywood proclaimed that sabotage was "the biggest, strongest and most wholesome weapon of the working class." Because the evidence was one man's word against another's, Haywood was acquitted in 1907.

As communism rose in Europe, Haywood hailed it as the redemption of the working class. Imprisoned in 1917 for his antiwar activities, he escaped while free on bond in 1921 and fled to Moscow, where he lived until his death in 1928 after suffering a stroke at the age of fifty-nine.

solution without prejudice to either party. He had made it clear that he opposed excess on the part of both labor and owners. Roosevelt hated the radical aggressiveness of many labor leaders. He did not wish to see closed shops, which are businesses where only members of specific unions can get jobs, since closed shops would limit employment opportunities for the average worker. But he also hated the excesses and wealth that had been achieved by breaking the backs of less fortunate small businesses or by abusing workers.

The Wobblies

The vast majority of laborers were willing to accept the slow but steady gains made through the efforts of unions such as the United Mine Workers or the American Federation of Labor. But some workers agitated

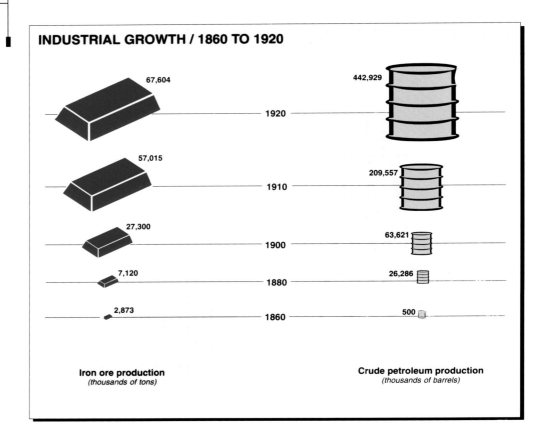

INDUSTRIAL GROWTH / 1860 TO 1920

67,604 — 1920 — 442,929

57,015 — 1910 — 209,557

27,300 — 1900 — 63,621

7,120 — 1880 — 26,286

2,873 — 1860 — 500

Iron ore production
(thousands of tons)

Crude petroleum production
(thousands of barrels)

This chart shows the staggering increase in iron ore and crude petroleum production in the U.S. from 1860-1920. Exports and imports also rose dramatically. By 1920 73 percent of workers were in occupations other than farming.

for more direct action. They drew together for a secret meeting in Chicago in 1905, and formed the Industrial Workers of the World (IWW), nicknamed the Wobblies. This group scorned the passive tactics of other groups and called for the emancipation of labor. The IWW drew its membership from the unskilled laborers, the migrants, the forgotten "red-blooded working stuff."

Under the leadership of "Big Bill" Haywood, an aggressive agitator, the IWW viciously attacked the policies of the American Federation of Labor and called for "abolition of the wage system." The IWW's following was small because of its left-wing stance and violent tactics. Nevertheless, the IWW's bent toward violence did draw attention to labor's problems.

The Industrial Trusts

Roosevelt's concerns about industrial power were significant because he was president during one of the most prosperous and industrially creative periods in American history. Production was increasing with each new industrial discovery, and vast natural resources were being uncovered. Roosevelt realized that big business held the only control over these new discoveries and resources; if there were no government controls or restrictions, workers' rights in large companies would be sacrificed for business profits.

He asked for the establishment of a Department of Commerce and Labor to investigate corporate earnings and protect workers' rights. His ideas were greeted warmly by the public; less enthusiastic party leaders recognized the turn in his path from party politics to reform.

Roosevelt turned his attention to trusts just three months after his 1901 speech to the Congress. Trusts were combinations of big businesses that controlled all or most of an industry. Some trusts were formed to increase efficiency through standardizing products or to gain other advantages not usually associated with competition. But other trusts had more sinister aims. By cornering the market for their product or service, they could eliminate price competition, allowing them to charge higher prices to their customers.

During the 1900s, many trusts had an arrangement whereby stockholders, often begrudgingly, transferred their voting power to a single group of trustees. Frequently, these trustees used their positions to line their own pockets. Today, these kinds of trusts are illegal in the United States.

Roosevelt Prosecutes the Trusts

Roosevelt disliked too much control by any special interests. As his name became synonymous with Progressivism, he acknowledged that the current laissez faire form of government — which had allowed big business and private interests free reign — needed some control. His alignment with the Progressives was solidified by his decision, in 1902, to regulate companies such as the Northern Securities Company.

The Northern Securities Company had been formed by J. P. Morgan and a number of the leading industrialists

from three main railroad lines that controlled rail transportation from Chicago to the West Coast. Roosevelt charged that this was in direct violation of the Sherman Antitrust Act, and the Supreme Court agreed with him, directing Morgan and his friends to break up this particular rail monopoly. But, in busting the Northern Securities Company, very little changed in the daily operations of the railroad. The few dominant railroad lines continued to operate with very little competition. Neither Morgan nor any other organizer of Northern Securities was jailed or paid significant fines for breaking a federal law. While the public saw Roosevelt as a hero protecting them

A 1905 cartoon by W. A. Rogers showing President Roosevelt leading the way in government control of monopolies and trusts. But he is being pulled from one direction by big business, in the form of Rockefeller, and from the other by reform, represented by William Jennings Bryan, former Democratic nominee for president and opponent of special privileges for the rich and powerful. In the background is James Jerome Hill of the Northern Securities Company, a trust which Roosevelt eventually busted.

John Pierpont Morgan. (1837-1913)

John Pierpont Morgan was born into his father's great wealth. His father, Julius, who had founded the Morgan financial empire with a dry goods firm, became a member of a London banking firm, and then opened his own banking firm of Dabney, Morgan and Company. The son was groomed to take over the firm upon Julius's retirement.

Under John's administration, the firm continued to flourish. In 1895, the young tycoon reorganized the company under the name J. P. Morgan & Company. One of Morgan's first tasks as head of this company was to end a gold shortage in the United States treasury by selling a $62 million government bond issue. By 1900, this firm was one of the leading companies financing businesses and marketing bond issues for the United States and British companies and governments.

After the Panic of 1893, Morgan helped reorganize many railroads, including the Northern Pacific, Erie, Southern, and the Philadelphia and Reading railroads, into the Northern Securities Company. In 1902, President Roosevelt chose this company as an example of a monopoly when he began trustbusting. When confronted with the possibility of being forced to dissolve the Northern Securities Company, Morgan reacted as though this could easily be resolved. He notified Roosevelt, "If we have done anything wrong, send your man to my man and they can fix it up."

Northern Securities was found guilty of violating the Sherman Antitrust Act and was dissolved. However, Morgan and the other organizers remained immensely powerful.

In 1901, J. P. Morgan helped establish U.S. Steel, the largest corporation to date in the United States. His company was also responsible for financing International Harvester, American Telephone and Telegraph, and General Electric. Morgan served as director of many of these corporations, as well as of banks, railroads, and other public utility companies and insurance firms.

To some, Morgan symbolized all that was good and great about the U.S. economic system. To others he was a robber baron, an aggressive monopolist using his monopoly privileges to drive up prices and drive down wages. Certainly, his great wealth and control of some of the biggest corporations in the country gave him great influence over all the politicians of the decade.

Many times, Morgan became involved in vicious stock battles to take control of smaller companies. The battles were at the expense of small stockholders — the elderly living on small pensions, or investors trying to capitalize on a company's profit. Morgan would negotiate and trade stocks short, often for half of their value. The pensioner and investor would end up with less than they had paid for stock shares, and Morgan would end up with a new company. He once said, "I owe the public nothing!" failing to recognize that it was the public's hard work that enabled him to own his vast business empire.

Throughout his life, Morgan donated money to education and charity. He gave substantial funds to build the Cathedral of St. John the Divine in New York City. He was also an avid art collector who, in one year alone, spent over $1 million on tapestries and scrolls. He donated many of his works of art to museums and libraries.

from a huge monopoly, the industrialists remained secure in their power.

Three years later, Roosevelt went after the Swift Company's beef trust. In this instance, a number of meat packers had formed a group to restrict the output of meat to raise their prices and obtain reduced railroad prices. On January 30, 1905, the Supreme Court ruled that the trust was acting in restraint of trade, in violation of the law.

Roosevelt Soft Pedals

Roosevelt also pursued corporations on the issue of granting rebates. Rebates were discounts or reductions of the amounts paid for services, for example, railroad freight charges. Sometimes rebates were given to obtain favors or good will. Generally, they were granted according to the amounts of goods shipped. But because of the huge amounts they shipped, large corporations or trusts were able to extract massive rebates. John D. Rockefeller's Standard Oil Company had secret deals with many of the railroad companies. The company even went so far as to demand that the railroads charge more to the company's competitors and then pay some of those higher charges back to Standard Oil! The smaller companies were powerless to compete. In 1907, the Standard Oil Company was fined $30 million for accepting rebates. This verdict was later set aside by a higher court.

Although appearing to be a man of action at times, Roosevelt was really soft peddling in his actions against monopolistic practices. Believing that big businesses were essential, he was reluctant in many ways to disturb the status quo. A humorist of the day made fun of Roosevelt's two-sided nature by putting these words in the president's mouth: "The trusts are hideous monsters built up by the enlightened enterprise of the men that have done so much to advance the progress of our beloved country.

An illustration of the global nature of John Pierpont Morgan's business schemes. In 1901, he bought Andrew Carnegie's steel company, merging it with several other firms to form the U.S. Steel Corporation, the first billion dollar company in U.S. history.

On the one hand I would stamp them under foot, on the other hand, not so fast."

During the Panic of 1907, Roosevelt was forced to turn to J. P. Morgan, the greatest monopolist of them all, to halt the collapse of share prices. Morgan had actually come to President Roosevelt with the dire warning that unless his firm, U.S. Steel, which had remained strong throughout the panic, took over the financially insolvent Tennessee Coal and Iron Company (TC & I), a number of banks and brokerage houses would collapse. The banks and brokerage houses had heavily invested their own funds, using TC & I stock as collateral. Morgan's plan was to replace TC & I stock collateral with U.S. Steel stock. But this purchase would turn U.S. Steel into a monopoly. Roosevelt was helpless to stop the impending disaster any other way, so he agreed to the sale of TC & I. Where once he had busted a Morgan trust, he was now helping to create one.

Promise of a Square Deal

In November 1904, Roosevelt was reelected after a rather boring campaign. At one point, Democratic nominee Judge Alton B. Parker accused Roosevelt of taking campaign contributions from special interest groups. Roosevelt responded that he was "unhampered by any pledge, promise or understanding of any kind, save as in my power lies I shall see to it that every man has a square deal, no less and no more."

In an era when laborers had no government support and no legal claim to jobs or benefits, Roosevelt made great strides toward government recognition of workers' rights. "The man is no true democrat . . . who, in problems calling for the exercise of a moral judgment, fails to take his stand on conduct and not on class," claimed Roosevelt when he favored the rights of the miners in the 1902 coal strike. Roosevelt believed that the rights of the laborers should be protected by the new Department of Commerce and Labor, and he opposed the use of the injunction — court orders prohibiting strikes — as "an engine of oppression against the wage-worker." But Roosevelt did not take his square deal so far as to favor unionization and, in most cases, followed a conservative policy toward labor.

Once he was reelected, Roosevelt declared that he would not seek another term in office. This freed him to make the promise of a square deal a reality, because he would not have to worry about pleasing the party bosses. The popular president set out to initiate reforms.

Roosevelt demanded legislation to curb railroad company abuses of the Elkins Act of 1903. This act made it illegal for railroads to return sums of money to favored shippers, thus helping smaller shipping companies remain in business. Because he no longer needed to be wary of those who put him in office, Roosevelt also focused on workers' and children's rights.

Muckraking

Roosevelt had help uncovering corporate abuses that needed correction. Investigative magazines such as *McClure's, Cosmopolitan, American Magazine*, and *Colliers* had been reporting abuse of workers, widespread corruption, and the misuse of land by businesses since the early 1900s. These magazines had a wide following among the public. Their reports were so frequent and popular that, in 1906, Roosevelt, tiring of the negative tone of many reports, labelled the magazines' reporters "muckrakers." The term had been picked up from John Bunyan's *Pilgrim's Progress*, which referred to laborers who raked the muck and never looked up from their tasks.

(Far right) Ida Tarbell was an author and muckraker who exposed the ruthless business methods of J. D. Rockefeller's Standard Oil Company in McClure's *magazine. Interviews with former Standard employees revealed that the company bought off politicians and devastated the environment in its search for crude oil.*

Roosevelt campaign buttons of 1904. One shows Roosevelt sitting at a table and drinking with an African-American — the first time that the idea of racial equality had appeared on a campaign button.

Whether or not he had tired of the investigations of the muckrakers, their reports were difficult to ignore. In 1902 and 1903, Lincoln Steffens had exposed government and police corruption in major cities in a series of articles that were later published as "The Shame of the Cities." Within the year, *McClure's* followed up with Ida Tarbell's exposé of the monopolistic and corrupt tactics of the Standard Oil Company, also later published as a book.

The muckrakers' efforts bore fruit and public outcry reached the president's office. The muckrakers were joined in their pleas for reform by many of the country's leading newspaper reporters, who took their roles so seriously that they had begun to form press clubs that served as social gathering spots and critical forums for each other's reporting. In New York, nightly gatherings for drink, talk, and often critical judgments of stories at "Doc" Perry's Park Row pharmacy had been going on since the late 1800s. The New York Press Club had been organized in 1873, and the National Press Club was organized in 1908. Reporting, especially muckraking, was becoming an esteemed occu-

pation in the 1900s world of political and social reform. Roosevelt recognized this medium's power, and many of his reforms were centered on correcting the abuses that the muckrakers and reporters observed and described.

The Food and Drug Act

It was thanks to one of the muckrakers that Roosevelt's administration was forced to intervene in the food industry. During the first decade of this century, there were widespread abuses in food and agricultural processing. Advertising burgeoned for patent medicines that did little to relieve illnesses and often contained merely alcohol. So Chief Chemist of the Department of Agriculture, Dr. Harvey W. Wiley, and his assistants acted as human guinea pigs to test foods and patent medicines. In 1904, they demonstrated that foods were often filled with preservatives such as formaldehyde and additives such as wood particles. The Food and Drug Act, which set limits on preservatives and established tests to determine the contents and benefits of patent drugs, passed the Senate early in 1906, but was caught up in House debates and not enacted as law until later that year.

The National Wholesale Liquor Dealer's Association lobbied hard against all food and drug legislation and threatened to boycott those newspapers that supported it. They may have won the battle if Upton Sinclair's novel, *The Jungle*, had not been published in 1906. In his reality-based novel, Sinclair depicted the extremes of American capitalism run amok. The book contained a section about a meat packing plant in which overworked and underpaid laborers were mistreated. It described spoiled and

"There would come all the way back from Europe old sausage that had been rejected, and that was moldy and white — it would be dosed with borax and glycerine, and dumped into the hoppers, and made over again for home consumption. There would be meat that had tumbled out on the floor, in the dirt and sawdust, where the workers had tramped and spit uncounted billions of consumption germs. There would be meat stored in great piles in rooms; and the water from leaky roofs would drip over it, and thousands of rats would race about on it."

Upton Sinclair,
The Jungle, 1906

Gifford Pinchot. (1865-1946)

In his autobiography, Theodore Roosevelt credited Pinchot with the responsibility for preserving America's natural resources. "He was the foremost leader in the great struggle to co-ordinate all our social and governmental forces in the effort to secure the adoption of a rational and far-seeing policy for securing the conservation of all our natural resources."

Born in Simsbury, Connecticut, Gifford Pinchot was the son of James Pinchot, a philanthropist, gentleman farmer, and businessman with a strong interest in forestry. Pinchot graduated from Yale University in 1889 and studied forestry in France, Germany, Switzerland, and Austria before entering the field at his father's suggestion in the United States. He wrote that he was taken with the idea because "the greatest, the swiftest, the most efficient, and the most appalling wave of forest destruction in human history was then swelling to a climax in the United States; and the American people were glad of it." Pinchot was referring to the Americans' beliefs that the forests were "inexhaustible and in the way" of development.

Gifford Pinchot, one of the first men to pursue conservation of natural resources, became a member of the National Forest Commission in 1896. He was responsible for setting aside thousands of acres of national forests for preservation. When the bureau grew to become the Forest Service of the U.S. Department of Agriculture in 1905, Pinchot served as its chief.

As a forester, Pinchot responded to America's obsession with development by encouraging Americans to make the forests perpetually productive. He believed the forests could be successfully utilized for both lumber and leisure. When he took on his greatest role as the nation's chief forester, Pinchot set about educating the public to manage forests and ranges, not just to preserve them. He encouraged tree farming techniques — or techniques combining harvesting and planting. He wrote with the conviction of a religious zealot of his and his service's role in conservation. "We were all young together, all eager, all proud of the division and all fiercely determined that its attack on forest devastation must win. We were ready to fight it out on this line if it took the rest of our lives. With such a cause and such a spirit we couldn't lose."

Pinchot became one of President Roosevelt's closest friends and part of the president's "tennis and riding cabinet," a group the president organized to work with him on the ideals of the "strenuous life" Roosevelt advocated. These activities included hiking, horseback riding, wrestling, and boxing. Pinchot once recalled that he often returned from these outings too exhausted to eat.

Pinchot was fired by President Taft in 1910 after he attacked Secretary of Interior Richard A. Ballinger for selling Alaska's mineral and coal lands to private interests and selling preserved lands cheaply.

filthy meat being ground into sausage, along with insects and rodent parts.

Sinclair had intended the novel to be a plea for socialism, but *The Jungle* quickly turned sentiments toward legislation that protected employees and consumers. An independent investigation by the Department of Agriculture supported Sinclair's descriptions. Upon learning the results of the investigation, Roosevelt put pressure on the House to pass the Meat Inspection Act, which was signed into law on June 23, 1906. The act authorized federal inspectors to examine meat shipped interstate and gave them the authority to enforce set standards for slaughterhouses. This act was hailed as a significant advancement for the public interest.

Environmental Concerns

Throughout his life, one issue burned in Roosevelt's heart. His early experiences as a rancher in the badlands of South Dakota had imbued in him a deep and abiding respect for the environment. So, long before it was a popular cause, Roosevelt took up the sword for conservation. His biggest supporter was Gifford Pinchot, the chief of the U.S. Forestry Service, part of the Department of Agriculture.

For decades, land had been passing out of government hands into private ownership. Forests, mineral deposits, and oil fields had been exploited. Roosevelt felt committed to limiting further destruction. As early as 1900, he

had supported the Lacey Act, making it a federal crime to illegally transport dead wild animals across state borders and limiting trade in bird feathers, animal imports, and the commercial killing of game.

Roosevelt supported the Newlands Reclamation Act of 1902, a federal reclamation program, which provided that the proceeds from land sales should be applied to the construction of dams and other works necessary to irrigate arid tracts. Settlers on the reclaimed lands were to repay the government, creating a revolving fund for irrigation projects. Projects included the Shoshone Dam in Wyoming and the Roosevelt Dam in Arizona. Under this plan, nearly 1.2 million acres were opened to cultivation by 1920.

Roosevelt's reclamation policies recycled and energized land; they also encouraged wildlife and game protection. He established the first wildlife refuge at Pelican Island, Florida. He also

Many ambitious irrigation projects, such as the Roosevelt Dam in Arizona, were begun after the passage of the Newlands Reclamation Act of 1902. Such schemes opened up over one million acres to cultivation by 1920.

withdrew 150 million acres of forest land from public sale and turned it into national forest, and, in 1903, he vetoed a bill awarding private interests the right to build a dam and generating system at Muscle Shoals in Alabama. Later, this site became the focus of debates over public versus private electrical power. In 1906, Roosevelt also removed millions of acres of coal and phosphate lands and water-power sites from public sale, saving them from over-exploitation.

Public Reaction

Because Roosevelt's support for conservation placed it in the spotlight, it became a popular issue. In 1908 in Washington, D.C., a conservation conference was held. Governors, legislators, scientific experts, and prominent citizens from all over the country united to formulate a declaration of principles urging the extension of forest fire services, protection for sources of navigable waterways, control of timber cutting on public and private land, and government intervention in subsoil rights (the rights to minerals found beneath the surface of the land), especially in coal, oil, and natural gas.

In response to this, forty-one state conservation commissions were established by 1909. To coordinate the commissions, Roosevelt appointed a National Conservation Commission with Pinchot acting as chair. Just before Roosevelt left office, a North American conference agreed to cooperate to preserve the natural resources of the continent.

Support for conservation was limited to a minority. Private interests stalled and attacked many efforts. Lumbering firms joined forces with oil companies and mining interests to

lobby against the new policy. Many western politicians opposed conservation because they feared it would retard growth in their districts. Congressmen resented the president's failure to gain legislative authorization for his commission and parts of his programs. Laws were passed in some states prohibiting further reservation of forest lands and denying funds for commissions. Despite this opposition, Roosevelt furthered public awareness and changed public opinion to support conservation, ensuring that no policies would be reversed once he left office.

A Miserable Job

In 1908, Roosevelt's appointee, Republican William Taft, a judge, corporate lawyer, and former governor of the Philippines, was elected president. Although historians claim Taft's administration to be adequate, he lacked the charm and showmanship of Roosevelt. He didn't know how to play his audience and quickly lost the support of Congress, while failing to grasp the heart of the American public. Though he busted more trusts during his four years in office than Roosevelt had in seven, Taft's administration signified, in many ways, a return to the old days. His cabinet was filled with men who retained ties with big business. He also dismissed Gifford Pinchot, Roosevelt's favorite, from the United States Forestry Service.

It should be noted that some reforms still did occur. Taft encouraged exploration — Americans Robert Edwin Peary and Matthew Henson made the first successful expedition to the North Pole during his administration — and demonstrated support for preservation of the nation's resources.

> *"We intend to use [the nation's] resources, but to use them so as to conserve them."*
>
> Roosevelt, on anouncement of the setting up of the National Conservation Commission, June 1908

Robert Edwin Peary. (1856-1920) and Matthew A. Henson. (1867-1955)

Born in Cresson, Pennsylvania, Robert Edwin Peary held a number of positions for various branches of the U.S. government, including draftsman, civil engineer, and survey developer. But it was his 1886 trip into the interior of Greenland — which, contrary to its name, is snow covered and freezing all year round — that began his lifelong fascination with the Arctic regions. Peary would spend the rest of his life trying to explore this land.

Peary called in the Philadelphia Academy of Natural Sciences to fund exploration in this area, but it took five long years of lobbying before he was placed in charge of research and exploration. By 1893, his research proved that Greenland was an island, and between 1893 and 1897, Peary uncovered scientific details about the nature of the polar region. He published his accounts in 1898 in *Northward Over the "Great Ice."*

In 1897, Peary took leave from his navy work to continue his explorations. His assistants, including Matthew Alexander Henson, traveled with him.

It was Henson, a black man born on a farm in Maryland, who became the most popular man with the Inuit (Eskimos) on the Arctic research teams, in part because he mastered the Inuit language and demonstrated proficient survival skills in the cold Arctic climate. In fact, Henson made all the sledges and stoves the research team used on their expeditions to the North Pole. A member of the Arctic expedition team recalled, "Henson, the colored man, went to the pole with Peary because he was a better man than any of his [Peary's] white assistants."

Peary and Henson made two exploratory expeditions to the north polar region in 1898 and 1905. In 1909, the party set out once again from Ellesmere Island. This time they were determined to reach the ultimate goal — the North Pole. As the group moved north, supplies ran low. One by one, members of the group turned back, until only four Inuit, Peary, and Henson remained. On April 6, 1909, the group reached a latitude of eighty-nine degrees, fifty-seven minutes. The men were just a few miles from the North Pole but were so exhausted they had to stop and rest a few hours before carrying on. They reached their destination the same day.

While at the North Pole, Peary and Henson took soundings and determined that, contrary to popular scientific belief at the time, the water around the North Pole is not a shallow body of water but actually quite deep. Peary wrote *The North Pole*, an account of this trip published in 1910. Many years later, Henson would publish his accounts in *A Negro Explorer at the North Pole*.

The first man to stand "on top of the world" was Henson. After the men planted the American flag on the North Pole, Peary refused to talk to Henson, most likely because he had been the first to reach the prized pole. Later, Peary prohibited Henson from showing slides or giving lectures about his experience. Because Henson's achievements were barely publicized, he worked as a porter, blacksmith, and messenger after leaving the research team and never received appropriate credit for his feat.

A few conservation laws were passed during this administration. For instance, although some of Alaska's land was sold to corporations, President Taft was given authority to withdraw other lands from private purchase and turn them over to forest preserves.

But Taft's advances were often stymied by an antagonistic Congress. He found his presidency to be lonely and long. Although he would run again, he secretly longed for the end of his life in public office. In fact, Taft was so miserable as president that when he turned the reigns of government over, he said to Woodrow Wilson, "I'm glad to be going. This is the lonesomest place in the world."

CHAPTER 5
Improvements in Medicine, Science, and the Home

Growing Cities and Crowded Conditions

Cities began to expand their boundaries into neighboring towns as the new middle class built Victorian-style homes at the edge of the streetcar line. (These may have been the first suburbs, but suburbs as we know them today didn't really take shape until after World War II.) Most cities sprang up around a hub that served as the main shopping area. But small cities within cities were formed when immigrants settled in areas where they could live among members of their own culture. These little cities had their own shopping centers where traditional foods could be purchased, and churches or temples where religious traditions could be followed.

Although some wealthy families lived in rural areas, most chose to live in the heart of their city to be close to shopping and cultural entertainment. The very rich owned a country or weekend home to complement their city lifestyle.

Factories were built along rivers and railroads because they relied on these resources for power and transportation. As industries grew, new housing sprang up around them. Sometimes these simple wood bungalows were built by factory owners who rented them at high cost to

their employees. Factory neighborhoods were the least desirable places to live in the cities because industrial waste produced soot, grime, and pollution that dusted the homes and choked the residents. When the middle and wealthy classes moved to the end of the streetcar line, they left behind housing that deteriorated as less well-to-do owners converted their homes into boarding houses. These were the first tenements, which were rented by new immigrants and displaced farm workers lured by new factories. As overcrowding worsened, open spaces between buildings were occupied by narrow apartments built by frugal businessmen, who exploited the housing shortage by squeezing as many small apartments as possible into these confined spaces.

These crowded conditions promoted diseases such as tuberculosis. Dozens of families shared facilities where germs bred easily. Many tenements lacked indoor bathrooms so tenants used public bath houses called natatoriums for bathing. Poorly paid workers could not provide nourishing food for their families. Doctors among the poor were few and far between. All these factors contributed to ill-health among the poor in urban centers.

The burgeoning cities were not equipped to respond to growing problems. Without enough police

> *"Not that they starve, but that they starve so dreamlessly, / Not that they sow, but that they seldom reap, / Not that they serve, but have no gods to serve, / Not that they die, but that they die like sheep."*
>
> Vachel Lindsay, poem about the urban poor

Washday in a tenement district of New York City. Wealthier people had moved out of city centers, leaving their large homes to be converted into boarding houses and rented out to the poorest in society. Crowded conditions and inadequate nutrition promoted disease.

officers and firefighters, crime and fires raged out of control. The murder rate increased from 1.2 per 100,000 in 1900 to 6.8 per 100,000 in 1920. Without enough garbage collectors, refuse piled up in the streets of the cities and polluted the drinking water.

Americans Fund Research

At the turn of the century, many scientists believed that science held the answers to the diagnosis of virtually all illness. Perhaps it could help with the illnesses created by poverty and overcrowding. Weapons to fight cancer and other diseases were already on the brink of discovery.

Researchers were helped along through the generosity of wealthy philanthropists, such as John D. Rockefeller, who gave $7 million to be used in research for a tuberculosis serum. With the help of the Rockefeller Institute for Medical Research, Dr. Wardell Stiles discovered the American species of hookworm in 1903 and began a campaign to eradicate the parasite. Andrew Carnegie founded the Carnegie Institute in Washington with $10 million to "encourage the broadest and most liberal manner of investigation, research and discovery, and the application of knowledge to the improvement of mankind."

But it is ironic that, in the final analysis, the money to provide the Rockefeller- and Carnegie-funded research largely came from the labor of the very people who were suffering from diseases and poor living

Andrew Carnegie is shown holding models of four of the many libraries that he endowed. Carnegie, who made his fortune in iron and steel, believed that those who gained great wealth had a responsibility to use some of it for the public good. Ironically, he and others like him had made their money in businesses that exploited the poor working class.

conditions. These magnates had become millionaires by manipulating ownership of the companies for which these immigrants toiled — companies where children worked very long hours for low pay, and where miners had no health or insurance benefits, and no right to strike for better conditions.

Public Health Advances

Gradually, these terrible conditions came to the attention of people with just enough power or will to do something about them. Preventive health programs were encouraged by some members of the health profession in America. A lone woman, Lillian Wald, furthered the cause of health reform for school children when, in 1902, she convinced the city of New York to hire school nurses to maintain student health and develop precautionary

education programs. Soon, other cities followed her lead and hired school nurses. Before the president's term ended, Wald had persuaded Theodore Roosevelt to support the establishment of the Federal Children's Bureau, which opened its doors in 1912. Funding for the bureau, which pioneered research on the relationship between the health of pregnant women and their babies, was granted in 1908.

In the southernmost part of America, Mary McLeod Bethune, a freed slave, fostered health and education reforms for blacks when she opened the Daytona Normal and Industrial School for Negro Girls in Daytona, Florida, in the fall of 1904. In order to get funding, this determined woman solicited help from some of the wealthiest industrialists and bankers in the country, including John D. Rockefeller and J.G. Gamble. Later, Bethune opened the first black hospital in Florida in the back of her school, in order to ensure medical care for her students and community.

Beriberi, rickets, and scurvy — all diseases now known to be caused by vitamin deficiency — had nagged humanity for centuries. Louis Pasteur and others had tried to find their cause, but to no avail. Frederick G. Hopkins, a British biochemist, discovered their secrets in 1906 when he demonstrated that substances contained in certain foods are vital for human growth and development. He called the substances "accessory food factors." They would later be called vitamins, and Hopkins' research would be used in the next decade to develop a theory that disease could be linked to vitamin deficiency.

John D. Rockefeller. (1839-1937)

At the age of twenty, John D. Rockefeller was a bookkeeper earning $40 a month. By the time he was twenty-six, he was a wealthy man and would ultimately die the richest man in America. Although Rockefeller was believed to be the world's first dollar billionaire, he could never verify this because he wasn't sure how much money he actually had.

John D. Rockefeller was born in Richford, New York, but grew up in a home of modest means in Cleveland, Ohio, where he attended high school and business college. During the Civil War, Rockefeller went into the produce business with M. B. Clark. The young men sold produce to the U.S. Army where they earned a reputation for honesty in business.

Rockefeller married Laura Spelman, the daughter of a Cleveland businessman. At twenty-six, he was the image of respectability, dressed in a frock coat and top hat, and was the local school superintendent where his wife taught Bible classes.

While running the produce business, some executives asked Rockefeller to see if there were any lucrative possibilities involved in the sinking of the first oil well. He reported that there were no possibilities, immediately bought his own oil refinery, and began making enough money to buy other refineries. By 1880, he controlled most of the world's oil markets. But he continued to be a frugal man who hated waste.

In fact, it was others' wasteful business practices, poor business sense, and misfortunes that probably helped to make Rockefeller so wealthy as he bought more and more refineries and turned them into large trusts. Critics said that to build up his business during the late 1800s, Rockefeller induced stockholders of over forty small companies to turn over their stock to nine trustees who would manage the trusts. The stockholders received trust certificates and a share in the trusts' profits, but no voice in the management. Before long, Rockefeller and his trustees owned enough refineries to control the oil business.

Rockefeller was also guilty of using unscrupulous business practices to obtain preferential shipping rates that his competitors couldn't match. After demanding that railways charge higher shipping prices to his competitors, he then forced them to pay him a bonus out of the extra charges.

The trusts became the Standard Oil Company, which soon expanded its activities in many directions. The company built pipelines, oil storage tanks, and laboratories to develop additional uses of oil's byproducts.

During the first decade of the twentieth century, Rockefeller's investments came under scrutiny. A deluge of court cases flowed against various Rockefeller companies. On January 14, 1907, Standard Oil of New Jersey was indicted on 539 counts for accepting rebates from the shipping companies. Two weeks later, the Interstate Commerce Commission published a report describing Standard Oil's methods of doing business as "a most scathing arrangement." On August 3 of that year, Standard Oil of Indiana was fined almost thirty million dollars for accepting rebates in violation of the Elkins Act. On May 19, 1907, the Commissioner of Corporations charged the Standard Oil Company with controlling transportation and maintaining a monopoly on the petroleum industry for thirty-five years. On January 1, 1908, a jury in Austin, Texas fined an affiliate, Waters Pierce Oil Company, over one and a half million dollars and advocated ousting Standard Oil from the state. In September 1908, Standard Oil was charged with violating the Sherman Antitrust Act, ultimately ending in the dissolution of the parent company. Roosevelt accused Standard Oil of "setting the pace in the race for wealth under illegal and improper conditions."

With all his wealth, ill-gotten or not, Rockefeller was also involved in charitable activities all his life. In 1908, he gave one million dollars to combat hookworm disease, and in 1913, he donated money to develop the Rockefeller Foundation "to promote the well-being of mankind throughout the world." The work of the foundation continues today.

Nurses training at Bellevue Hospital, New York, look at bacteria under a microscope. Advances in biochemistry and microbiology were leading to the discovery of the causes of disease and to ways of fighting it. Already antibodies had been grown in test tubes and vitamins had been discovered. Yet both the nursing profession and that of doctors remained largely segregated by gender, and few women became doctors.

Scientific Advances

Finding scientific answers to the mysteries of viruses and other diseases would increase people's odds of survival. Yellow fever had been the scourge of the South and the Caribbean for centuries. In June 1900, a Yellow Fever Commission was appointed to eradicate the deadly disease in Cuba. Major William Crawford Gorgas and Dr. Walter Reed worked together to exterminate the deadly disease. The scientists set out to investigate a theory put forth by the Cuban doctor, Carlos Finley, that mosquitoes caused yellow fever.

The doctors established a sanitary station and placed healthy persons in the midst of yellow fever victims. They were able to prove that their subjects remained healthy unless they were bitten by infected mosquitoes. The cause of yellow fever was determined. On December 20, 1900, Reed wrote to his wife: ". . . it has been permitted to me and my assistants to

Mary McLeod Bethune. (1875-1955)

Mary McLeod was born into a family of seventeen children in Mayesville, South Carolina on July 10, 1875. Her parents were freed slaves and the family lived in a log cabin on five acres of farmland. Despite the family's meager existence, she was raised in an atmosphere of love and generosity.

As a child, she worked alongside her parents, sisters, and brothers, picking cotton, cultivating a vegetable garden, fishing for eels and mullet, and hunting rabbit, possum, and quail. At the age of seven, she attended the Trinity Presbyterian Church School and graduated in 1886. A bright and eager student, she put what she had learned to use and helped neighbors to calculate weights and prices on the scales at the local cotton gin.

McLeod Bethune's early experiences of helping the needy drove her to consider a life as a missionary. At the age of twelve, she received a scholarship to Scotia Seminary for black women in Concord, North Carolina. McLeod Bethune worked as a housemaid to pay for room and board. When she completed her education, she discovered there were no openings in African missions, her original goal. She became a missionary in her own country when she returned to her home to help Emma Wilson, the Presbyterian school's founder, run the school. In May 1898, she married Albertus Bethune, and in February 1899, she bore a son, Albertus.

In 1904, McLeod Bethune learned that many black laborers were constructing the Florida East Coast Railway in Daytona Beach. She decided to follow the example of Wilson and begin her own school in Daytona Beach.

She founded the Daytona Normal School and Industrial Institute for Negro Girls in a two-story cottage near the railroad tracks with five girls who paid fifty cents a week for tuition. Over the entrance to the school, McLeod Bethune posted the school motto: "Enter to Learn. Depart to Serve." Rent was $11 per month, and some students boarded with McLeod Bethune when their mothers, who worked as maids, went away with their employers for the summer.

McLeod Bethune was often challenged in her decision to run a school for African-American women. The Ku Klux Klan objected to blacks learning to read and write and threatened her school and students. Some African-Americans fought the school because they feared the KKK's threats and violence and thought to avoid them by closing the school. But McLeod Bethune stood up to the KKK and continued to run her school with donations and the small tuition fee she collected.

When the school outgrew its two-story cottage, John D. Rockefeller and John Gamble, the cofounder of Procter and Gamble, helped McLeod Bethune buy land and build a larger school. But it was always a precarious existence. Neighbors helped erect the new school, many exchanging labor for tuition. Thomas H. White, the owner of the White Sewing Machine Company, became a lifelong friend and a supporter of the school, supplying sewing machines, blankets, and even a coat for McLeod Bethune when he saw how threadbare hers was.

In 1908, the same year Booker T. Washington visited the school, the growing male enrollment prompted McLeod Bethune to change the school's name to the Daytona Educational Industrial Training School. She explained to Washington that when someone said something was impossible, she simply responded, "Go ahead and do it."

lift the impenetrable veil that has surrounded the causation of this most dreadful pest of humanity and to put it on a rational and scientific basis. I thank God that this has been accomplished during the latter days of the old century. May its cure be wrought in the early days of the new!"

In February, 1901, the report of the Yellow Fever Commission was read at the Pan-American Medical Congress at Havana. Major Gorgas

Dr. Walter Reed. (1851-1902)

As a student, Walter Reed was described as a gifted, hard-working young man. He challenged himself at every turn, earning his first medical degree at the age of seventeen from the University of Virginia School of Medicine. When Reed discovered that patients had trouble trusting such a youthful physician, he decided to obtain a second degree at Bellevue Hospital in New York to bide his time until he was old enough to be taken seriously as a doctor. After graduating, he worked as a medical inspector in Brooklyn and won a commission in the U.S. Army Medical Corps. He married Emilie Lawrence in 1876, and the couple had two children.

Reed was appointed to the Yellow Fever Commission in 1900, to investigate the causes of the disease. Reed, who had already discovered the cause of typhoid, loved his work and welcomed the challenge of finding yellow fever's cause. Upon his arrival in Cuba, the doctor tested blood samples and cultures in an effort to determine the microbe that was causing the disease. He found nothing. He stood by helplessly as eighty-five out of every hundred people who contracted yellow fever died.

Then, Reed recalled that a Cuban physician, Dr. Carlos J. Finley, believed that the mosquito was responsible for carrying the disease. Reed and his team realized they would have to allow mosquitoes to bite healthy men after biting victims of the disease in order to determine if this were, in fact, the cause of the dreaded disease.

But Reed's work was filled with controversy. Although fourteen American soldiers volunteered to be bitten by mosquitoes to contract yellow fever, more volunteers were needed. Reed and his colleagues began to frequent the Tiscornia Immigration Station in Cuba. The men would pick about ten healthy men from the groups of new arrivals and hire them to work at the testing site.

The Spanish immigrants, who were housed in mosquito-proofed tents and fed well, were instructed to pick up loose stones around the experimentation camp. They were encouraged to take their time and rest often. Meanwhile, Reed and his associates questioned the workers closely to determine those who were in poor medical condition, who had previously suffered yellow fever, or who had dependent relatives. These men were excused from the camp. The rest were offered $100 to become volunteers. If they contracted the disease, they were promised an additional $100. The money seemed an incredible sum to the island immigrants, and most signed on immediately.

On November 21, 1900, a Havana newspaper heard about the human experiments. It carried a brutal editorial attack against the Yellow Fever Commission, condemning the Americans as heartless for taking advantage of the poor immigrants. But the Spanish consul in Cuba responded by giving his blessing, saying that any measure, no matter how dangerous, was acceptable to eradicate yellow fever. Reed's experiments, made public in February 1901, proved that a particular type of mosquito that bred in standing water was responsible for the spread of yellow fever.

Reed died of a ruptured appendix on November 23, 1902, at the age of fifty. Inscribed above his grave in Arlington National Cemetery are the words, "He gave man control over that dreadful scourge, yellow fever."

pledged to rid the country of the disease-carrying mosquito which, he had discovered, preferred to lay its eggs in clean water. A campaign began in which inspectors went door to door examining water receptacles. A film of oil was poured over water in wells, cisterns, water barrels, and cesspools. This suffocated the larvae when they came to the top. By the end of 1901, yellow fever had been eradicated from Havana. Typhoid also disappeared from Cuba as a result of these sanitation measures.

Chemical Disease Fighters

Meanwhile, the search for a treatment and cure for other killer diseases was on. Dr. Paul Ehrlich was working on the development of serum therapy that would eventually lead to chemotherapy, or the use of chemical compounds, to fight disease. By mid-1900, Ehrlich had successfully grown antibodies in test tubes. These tiny one-celled animals fought diseases for which the human body was unable to produce natural antibodies. In 1908, Ehrlich received the Nobel Prize in Medicine for his research.

In 1900, syphilis was — as it still is — one of America's greatest health threats. By the early twentieth century, doctors reported that the country's mental institutions were filled with patients whose mental illnesses were late-stage syphilitic infections. One physician suggested, "The elimination of these diseases would render one-third, possibly one-half, of our institutions for defectives unnecessary." In 1910, Ehrlich announced his discovery of a chemical that killed

the spirochete, the germ that caused syphilis. "Salvarsan," or safe arsenic, used to kill the spirochete, was actually the first form of chemotherapy.

While some scientists researched into the treatment of disease, others were fascinated with the secrets of human development. In 1900, a document written by Hugo Vries of Holland and Carl Correns of Germany outlined the first laws of inheritance, which were discovered through tracking the dominant and recessive genes passed on from parents to their children. An international team of researchers including Vries and Correns, as well as Erich Tschermak of Austria-Hungary, and a Benedictine monk, Gregor Johann Mendel, discovered the genes for things such as hair and eye color, as well as those that pass on inherited strengths and weaknesses.

Probing the Psyche

The human mind and its secrets also came under study during this decade. Around the world, psychologists and neurologists were busy trying to understand the reasons for human behavior. One neurologist in particular was about to change the theory of the mind forever.

Sigmund Freud, the famous Viennese doctor, developed a theory of personality that suggested that the unconscious mind controls actions, that humans are instinctive creatures, and that childhood experiences have tremendous impact on adult behavior. To unlock the hidden messages that dictate human behavior, Freud developed psychoanalysis — the talking out or free association of ideas. Until Freud, doctors had used a combina-

"The prayer that has been mine for twenty years, that I might be permitted in some way or at some time to do something to alleviate human suffering, has been granted!"

Dr. Walter Reed

Sigmund Freud (seated, far left) and Carl Jung (seated, far right) during Freud's lecture tour of America in 1909. It was a decade of conflicting views on the workings of the human mind. After hearing Freud, one listener said, "Freud advocates free love, a removal of all restraints and a relapse into savagery."

tion of hypnosis and talking out, but did not delve into a patient's past or subconscious mind as Freud did.

Calling his theory the "Theory of the Unconscious Mind," Freud also developed the idea of the id, ego, and superego to describe the three distinct parts of the mind. The id, he said, demands pleasure, while the ego makes rational behavior possible. The superego is the mind's conscience. Freud published *The Interpretation of Dreams*, which explained his theories, in 1900. In this text, he analyzed his own and others' dreams and demonstrated how conflicts between the id and ego come out in dreams. The book helped the untrained person understand the elements of psychotherapy and contained a strong emphasis on sexual instinct. It made Freud a household name.

On September 10, 1909, Freud brought his theories to the United States at a conference at Clark University in Worcester, Massachusetts. Of psychology's popularity, Freud said, "It seemed like the realization of some incredible daydream: psychoanalysis was no longer a product of delusion, it had become a valuable part of reality."

But not everyone applauded Freud's theories. Alfred Adler, an early associate of Freud's, believed that Freud's stress on sexual instinct was inaccurate. The primary drive, according to Adler, was superiority or overcoming childhood feelings of being inferior. He coined the term "inferiority complex."

Carl Gustav Jung, of Switzerland, who befriended Freud in 1907, also challenged Freud in many areas. Jung defined the libido as the will to live. After working with Pueblo Indians, he developed the theory of the collective unconscious, in which the unconscious was thought to comprise inherited memory mixed with individual experience. Jung thought that patients should work through current conflicts rather than those from childhood. Calling application of his theories analytical psychology, Jung classified personality types as introverted and extroverted. His theories were so far removed from Freud's that the friendship between the two men ended in 1913.

Exploring the Elements

Other scientists were exploring the physical world in which the human animal lived. A Polish scientist, Marie Curie, was fascinated by the discovery that uranium salts gave off a luminescence even in the absence of light. She wondered what new or undiscovered element was responsible. Using the electrometer that Pierre Curie, her French husband and a fellow researcher, had invented to measure the results of his own research, Curie began to determine the undiscovered elements in these unusual rays.

Because uranium metal was obtained from pitchblende, a uranium oxide ore, and only traces of the element that produced luminescence

Marie Curie worked with radioactive materials to discover two new elements, plutonium and radium. These eventually revolutionized the diagnosis and treatment of disease, especially cancer.

were found in uranium, Curie obtained a ton of the ore. In a leaky, unheated shed behind the girls' school in Paris where she taught, she began the tedious task of separating the elements. By 1898, she had separated out enough elements from the pitchblende to have a trace of powder that measured four hundred times more radioactive than uranium. She called her discovery "polonium" after her native land, Poland.

At this point, her husband abandoned his own research and began working with her. Eventually, in 1902, the Curies separated another more radioactive element from the polonium. They announced the discovery of the new element, which they called "radium."

The Curies' findings were finally published in 1903, when Marie Curie presented her doctoral thesis for her Ph.D. Her work was recognized with the 1903 Nobel Prize in Physics, which also named fellow researchers Pierre Curie and Henri Becquerel for their studies in uranium radiations. Another Nobel Prize for Curie would follow in 1911, and radium would lead the way in diagnosis of disease and the fight against cancer. However, she never lived to see this. Marie Curie had discovered that radium had a darker side — she died of leukemia in 1934.

Einstein and Rutherford

It is probable that one particular German scientist paid close attention to the Curies' and Ehrlich's work. He may have wondered if his own scientific theories would ever be recognized or accepted. It is likely that he was encouraged by their findings and so was motivated to carry on his own research. Until 1905, Albert Einstein worked as the examiner of patents in Bern, Switzerland. But that fateful year, at the age of twenty-six, he published his *Theory of Relativity*, which demonstrated that matter and energy were different aspects of the same thing. Matter, the theory stated, could be converted into energy and energy could be converted into matter. As a result of his studies, in 1909, Einstein was hired as a researcher at the prestigious University of Prague.

Others were also recognized for their contributions during this decade. In 1908, a New Zealand-

Albert Einstein's theories about the nature of the universe were conceived during this decade, but it would be some time before his ideas brought him worldwide fame.

born Canadian scientist named Ernest Rutherford received the Nobel Prize in Chemistry for his research on the structure of the atom. Earlier, in 1899, Rutherford had discovered the mathematical rate at which radioactive substances break down. By 1908, he was detecting subatomic particles by shooting atoms at a zinc sulfide screen to produce a tiny flash. Before the middle of the twentieth century, Rutherford's knowledge demonstrated that these particles could be controlled. His discoveries would later be used to turn radioactivity into a useful scientific tool.

Science and Improvements in Farming

While medical minds during this decade developed new theories and practices to help people live longer and happier lives, technological minds made living easier and more comfortable.

George Washington Carver, an African-American botanist, spent this decade teaching agriculture at Tuskegee Institute, the black college founded by Booker T. Washington. Carver, the son of a slave who was adopted by a white couple after his mother was kidnapped, developed a rotation system for crops in the cotton-growing regions. The system included planting peanuts and sweet potatoes to replenish soil after its nutrients had been depleted by years of cotton growing. When peanuts and sweet potatoes became plentiful, Carver developed new uses for them. He developed over three hundred synthetic byproducts from peanuts, including soap, cheese, and dyes. From the sweet potato, 118 synthetic byproducts could be extracted, including molasses, paste, and rubber. Carver also introduced the soybean to American farmers when he brought it to the United States from China. He discovered that soybeans replace the nitrogen in poor soil as they grow.

Home Developments

Research wasn't limited to the scientific and health fields. It entered the average American's home, and although it may have needed some fine tuning, it made life easier, especially for the country's homemakers.

Middle-class housewives must have been intrigued when they heard that Westinghouse had begun manufacturing electric irons and toasters. They must have choked on their enthusiasm when they discovered that the irons were large and heavy, more useful in commercial establishments than in their homes. They were more likely to use the first toasters, which were smaller than the irons, but a far cry from the slim pop-up models in use by the middle of the century. The earliest electric toasters were bread presses with electric coils along each side. They cooked the toast unevenly and could only be used under a watchful eye. Unless the user remembered to open them and pull out the toasted bread, it would burn to a crisp. Help was usually hired in middle-class and wealthier homes, so many homeowners bought these products and then left it to their domestic servants to figure them out.

George Washington Carver. (1864?-1943)

George Washington Carver revitalized the dying agriculture of the South when he developed a system of crop rotation to rejuvenate soil that had been depleted by years of planting cotton. When the peanuts and sweet potatoes that he recommended became plentiful, he went on to develop synthetic uses for the crops.

Born of slave parents on Moses Carver's plantation in Diamond Grove, Missouri, George Washington Carver and his mother were kidnapped while he was still an infant. Although his mother was never recovered, he was ransomed for a horse by his owner.

Carver worked his way through high school in Minneapolis and, in 1891, he entered Iowa Agricultural College, now called Iowa State University in Ames, Iowa. He was given an appointment as the first African-American to serve on the school's faculty, where he taught agriculture and bacterial biology while pursuing graduate work. He continued to paint as a hobby, and in 1893, four of his paintings were exhibited at the World's Fair Columbian Exposition. In 1896, Carver received his master's degree in agriculture after publishing papers about the prevention of certain fungus diseases that destroyed cherry trees, currant bushes, and other plants like wheat, oats, and barley. Over his lifetime, Carver discovered at least four fungus growths that attacked different plants.

In 1896, Carver took a position at Tuskegee Normal and Industrial Institute for Negroes. Here, he took barren land and planted legumes, such as cow peas, to add nitrates to the soil. The legumes enriched the soil as they grew. After the cow peas were harvested, Carver planted sweet potatoes, then cotton. By the time the cotton was planted, the soil was so enriched that the cotton yield per acre was outstanding.

Carver told farmers, "Plant peanuts. They are excellent legumes, they enrich the soil, they are easy to plant, easy to grow, and easy to harvest; they are rich in protein and good for feeding livestock, they yield a high percentage of oil of a superior quality. A pound of peanuts contains a little more nutrients than a pound of sirloin steak."

Soon, warehouses were overflowing with peanuts. Carver developed 325 different products from peanuts, including cream, coffee, face powder, ink, shampoo, vinegar, dyes and wood stains. Industries to make these products sprang up, and the South began to prosper.

Carver then turned his attention to sweet potatoes and produced 118 products, including ink, starch, flour, tapioca, dyes, and synthetic rubber. During World War I, the U.S. Army used Carver's sweet potato mix with wheat flour to make bread.

Carver also found seventy-five uses for the pecan and developed hundreds of products from corn stalks. When cotton became over-abundant because of Carver's soil rotation plans, he developed byproducts, including insulating board, rugs, cord, and highway paving blocks to make better use of the entire crop.

The first electric vacuum cleaners were developed about 1900. By 1908, Hoover vacuum cleaner salesmen were filling their pockets with profits by selling door to door.

Washing machines had been invented in 1860 by Hamilton E. Smith of Philadelphia. Housewives' burdens weren't really eased much by these devices, however. To operate the washing machine, the women needed to turn a hand crank to rotate paddles inside a metal tub. These paddles pushed the laundry through water. Depending on the machine design, the women then had to remove laundry from the tub and pass it through two rollers called a wringer to squeeze out excess moisture. Then laundry was replaced in the tub, which had been filled with clean water, to be rinsed, passed through the wringer again, and hung to dry. An electric machine was finally developed about 1910, freeing housewives just a little

more. Although they no longer needed to stand at the machine to turn the crank, they still had to wring clothes and change the water manually.

These appliances were intended to help homemakers perform their primary duty, to keep the house running smoothly. A popular home health guide advised, "Home must be a place of repose, of peace, of cheerfulness, of comfort," then a husband's soul "renews its strength and will go forth with fresh vigor to encounter the labor and troubles of the world."

This advertisement shows a domestic servant using a vacuum cleaner, a new invention in the early 1900s. Middle-class and wealthy homeowners generally had servants to do the housework. The less well-off could not afford help, nor such labor-saving devices.

Frederick Taylor. (1856-1915)

Frederick Taylor, nicknamed "Speedy" because of his work, was an American engineer and efficiency expert who spent the late 1800s conducting experiments to determine the maximum efficiency of people and machines at the Midvale Steel Works in Philadelphia. His time and motion study, called "the stopwatch and clipboard approach," became part of a highly detailed system of organizing and systemizing factory work.

Taylor's theory was to analyze a task and break it down into its basic motions. Individual workers' tasks could then be simplified into elemental skills and reorganized in minute detail by using plans drafted by engineers. Physical labor and stress were effectively reduced by eliminating wasted motions, and the pace of work was increased. Taylor also recommended that management isolate workers to avoid "time-wasting" habits such as socializing. He promised factory managers that they would increase productivity and profits, and promised laborers higher wages based upon their increased efficiency.

Officially called "Taylorism," the system led to the development of many analytical approaches to production used by a number of American factories during the early 1900s. The engineer lived Taylorism in his personal life, inventing a device that woke him if he fell asleep in his chair.

Taylor designed charts to analyze factory operations. Two that are still used today are the "elemental breakdown form," which studies the different steps taken to produce an item and times each step using a stopwatch, and the "left hand-right hand" chart, which studies the motions of a single operator at work. The stopwatch study was originally used to set standards of labor output to achieve a "fair day's pay for a fair day's work."

Taylor gave a number of lectures in Detroit between 1900 and 1909. In fact, in 1909, Taylor made a four-hour speech to Packard management about his time and motion studies that is said to have changed car production theories forever.

Taylor's theories gained tremendous popularity in American factories, especially after Henry Ford began using them profitably. But Ford took these theories a step further. He decided that machines could run more efficiently than humans and so began to study the feasibility of mechanized assembly-line production.

After 1910, Taylor became known as the "Father of Scientific Management." In 1911, he published *The Principles of Scientific Management*, further publicizing the way scientific management techniques could be used throughout the United States.

Food Production and the Canning Industry

With the growth of a middle class came middle-class consumption. A country of entrepreneurs eager to market their wares welcomed each new customer with new and unusual products, especially new foods.

For instance, a sugary, rubber-textured dessert that came in just about any flavor a child could desire was introduced in 1902 when Pearl Wait developed Jello. In 1906, Will Keith Kellogg, "the king of the cornflakes," brought new production theories to the food industry when he opened his cereal company. Kellogg may be remembered for his extensive cereal empire, but the man should also be acknowledged for his master salesmanship. His advertising campaigns convinced a nation of families that grain products, found in his Cream of Wheat and Corn Flakes, were a healthier breakfast than meat and eggs.

Factories that produced items for middle-class consumption were changing, too, even ones that produced foodstuffs. At least one researcher focused on efficiency in the workplace during this decade. Frederick W. Taylor, an American engineer and efficiency expert, had spent the last years of the nineteenth century conducting experiments to analyze the maximum efficiency of people and machines at the Midvale Steel Works in Philadelphia. His time and motion study eventually led to a detailed system for organizing and systemizing factory operations. Called "Taylorism," the system was used in many American factories during the early 1900s. Not everyone was happy with "scientific management," as the system was also known. Workers felt cheated and angry at the work speedups. However, efficiency became a popular watchword or obsession that was also used in many endeavors outside the factory, like city management and sports.

The nation's farmers soon caught on to the fact that if they used improved production techniques, their land would yield bigger crops. If they could then figure out a way to preserve and package these harvested crops, they could cash in on the more profitable mass production market. The idea of turning farming into a production industry spawned the canning industry. Gail Borden had been using canning techniques to package condensed milk for city consumption since 1860, but now apples and corn,

potatoes and carrots, even squash and pumpkins were gathered by local farmers to be sold to a local canning company. There they were cooked, canned, packaged, and shipped to the country's cities and towns for distribution in the corner grocery stores.

The average American discovered new products everywhere. They ranged from the silly to the sublime, the ridiculous to the practical. What a time it must have been for experimenting and exploring. But it was just the beginning. Who knew what would be invented tomorrow?

Increasing crop yields led to attempts to preserve food, and so the canning industry began. Farmers sold their harvests to canning companies, where the food was processed. From there, canned goods were sent to grocery stores in every town and city.

CHAPTER 6
The Transportation Revolution

America of 1900 held great promise for dreamers and visionaries. Eccentric geniuses and creative mechanics tinkered in their garages on their versions of the ultimate vehicle to replace the horse. Some would develop just a single automobile for their own use; others thought beyond that to affordability and mass production; a few looked to the sky and wondered what it would be like to take wing. Two bicycle repairmen from Dayton, Ohio, aligned themselves with these few. They discovered they could soar.

The Wright Stuff

Wilbur and Orville Wright were fascinated with the thought of powered flight. They contacted the Smithsonian Institution and obtained all the scientific data gathered by Otto Lilienthal of Germany, a pioneer in gliding who made close to two thousand flights before he died in a plane crash on August 10, 1896. They researched other air pioneers as well. By 1899, the Wright Brothers had designed and built a five-foot biplane kite.

On the advice of the Weather Bureau, now the National Weather Service, the brothers went to Kitty Hawk, North Carolina, where conditions for flight appeared perfect.

Here, a dune-covered beach, part of a series of islands called the Outer Banks, jutted out along the Carolina coastline. The dunes were high enough to give the brothers the momentum they needed. Although the islands were subject to bitter winter rain storms, it was pleasantly brisk most of the year. The steady wind would get them airborne. In 1900, the Wrights flew their first pilot-flown glider from Kill Devil Hill, the tallest dune in Kitty Hawk. This glider had a sixteen-foot wingspan and cost $15 to build. Wilbur flew several feet for a matter of a few seconds before he and the glider made a bumpy return to the ground.

Wilbur and Orville were thrilled with this short but promising experience. They spent the winter experimenting with designs in the back of their bicycle shop. The brothers discovered errors in Lilienthal's research when they set up a six-foot wind tunnel in their home. Using the tunnel they redesigned the wings' curved surfaces. They returned to Kitty Hawk in 1901 with a larger glider, designed with guide wires to give them some control of sideways movement. Again, they flew the glider for only short distances. The brothers were encouraged by the control the guide wires provided but wanted to fly higher and further. They returned to Dayton to find a way to

Wilbur Wright. (1867-1912) and Orville Wright. (1871-1948)

Wilbur Wright was born near Millville, Indiana and Orville in Dayton, Ohio, where they spent most of the rest of their lives. The boys grew up experimenting with toy-making and building their own wagons to haul rags to the junkman to pay for their supplies. By the time they were teenagers, Wilbur had set up his own printing business, edited the church bulletin, and ran a newspaper, the *West Side News*, out of his house. Just before high school graduation, Wilbur dropped out to stay home and nurse his mother, who was dying of tuberculosis, while Orville continued school and ran the print shop.

By 1892, the brothers were interested in both bicycle and automobile development. They were kept so busy repairing bicycles that they decided to open their own shop. They put their assistant, Ed Sines, in charge of the print shop and went into the bicycle business as The Wright Bicycle Company. The business grew rapidly, and before long, they moved to larger quarters.

By 1899, the brothers were working on a new interest — the flying machine. "Our own growing belief that man might . . . learn to fly," wrote Wilbur to a friend, "was based on the idea that while thousands of the most dissimilar body structures, such as insects, reptiles, birds and mammals were flying every day at pleasure, it was reasonable to suppose that man might also fly."

In 1900, the brothers went to Kitty Hawk, North Carolina, to fly their first piloted glider. Their best glides that year lasted fifteen to twenty seconds and covered three hundred to four hundred feet.

Each summer over the next few years, the brothers experimented in the back of their bicycle shop with wind tunnels, wing shapes, and engines. Each fall, they returned to Kitty Hawk. By 1902, the brothers had designed a fully controlled glider. In 1903, they returned to Kitty Hawk with a gasoline-powered airplane. "Isn't it astonishing that all these secrets have been preserved for so many years just so that we could discover them!" Orville told a friend.

Back at home in Dayton, the brothers issued a press statement. It read: "As winter was already well set in, we should have postponed our trials to a more favorable season, but . . . we were determined before returning home, to know whether the machine possessed sufficient power to fly, sufficient strength to withstand the shock of landings, and sufficient capacity of control to make flight safe in boisterous winds, as well as in calm air. When these points had been definitely established, we at once packed our goods and returned home, knowing that the age of the flying machine had come at last."

The press was beginning to pay attention, and Wilbur grew concerned that the design for the unpatented invention would be stolen. So, while the brothers waited for their patent application to be accepted, they worked secretly at Huffman Prairie in Dayton, Ohio. Their patents were approved in 1906, and the brothers made headlines as they demonstrated flight openly once again.

In 1909, Wilbur and Orville opened the doors to their own manufacturing company and began producing Wright Flyers in Dayton. Although they would always be in the center of flight, the two brothers would never again be at the forefront of the industry. Rather, they spent the rest of their years fighting patent infringement suits.

obtain the lifting power they needed to get the glider off the ground and maintain it in the air.

In 1902, the Wrights returned to Kitty Hawk with an aerodynamically advanced glider. That year, they made one thousand glides, some as far as six hundred feet. They were on the verge of designing a world-changing invention, and they were going further and further each year.

The brothers needed to protect their designs. They applied for a patent in 1903, which was accepted in 1906. Until then, they continued to experiment but shied away from publicity and attention.

A Wing-warping System

It wasn't until December 17, 1903 that the Wright Brothers were able to take a powered flying machine into the air. The biplane, made of a wood frame with sateen-covered wings, carried a single pilot who lay prone in the middle of the bottom wing. The gasoline-powered engine on the pilot's right turned two wooden propellers located behind the wings. The pilot controlled the wing-warping (or wing-twisting) system with guide wires near his feet. The brothers called their biplane *The Flyer* and were ecstatic when it proved to be capable of flight!

In 1904, the brothers flew 105 flights, totaling only forty-five minutes in the air. But each flight taught them a little more and helped them improve on their original designs. On October 5, 1905, their airplane flew 24.2 miles in thirty-eight minutes, three seconds. The brothers were so enthused by their success that they contacted the U.S. government about buying their designs. Much to their chagrin, the government refused to take the flying machine seriously. It wasn't until 1908 that the Wright

The world's first controlled, piloted, motor-propelled flight. Orville Wright lies face down in the middle of the bottom wing and pilots the biplane with guide wires near his feet. This flight was the culmination of several years' research into a suitable design. It was years before the U.S. government saw the practical uses of a flying machine.

Brothers closed a contract with the U.S. Department of War for the first military airplane.

They continued to experiment and improve on their designs. Wilbur went to France, where exhibition flights at a height of over three hundred feet so impressed the French that they contracted with the brothers to build a number of planes. Meanwhile, Orville made exhibition flights in the United States. On September 9, 1908, over the drill field at Fort Myers, Virginia, he made fifty-seven complete circles at an altitude of 120 feet, remaining in the air for one hour and two minutes.

Their accomplishments were tempered with some disasters, though. On September 17, Orville crashed during an exhibition in Virginia, suffering a broken thigh and two broken ribs. It took the better part of a year for him to recover. His passenger, Thomas E. Selfridge, died.

In August 1909, the Wright Brothers signed a contract with a German company to create the German Wright Company. In November of that year, the brothers also formed the U.S.-based Wright Company. Despite obtaining a patent on their designs, the Wright brothers were troubled by imitators and spent many years in the courts, fighting to maintain patent rights over their designs.

Many other inventors followed the Wright Brothers' lead. On July 4, 1908, Glenn Curtiss made a flight of just over a mile in his third plane, *June Bug*. But Curtiss then became embroiled in a patent infringement lawsuit with the Wright brothers because his plane used a wing-warping system similar to one the brothers had developed. In 1909, the Frenchman,

Louis Bleriot, became the first pilot to fly across the English Channel. John A. D. McCurdy, a Canadian engineering student, made the first successful

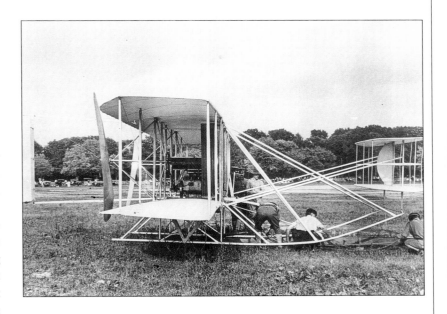

Canadian flight on February 23, 1909, when he flew his biplane more than half a mile across Bras d'Or Lake in Nova Scotia.

Speaking of the possibilities of flight, Wilbur Wright once said, "When my brother and I built and flew the first man-carrying flying machine, we thought that we were introducing into the world an invention which would make further wars practically impossible." Unfortunately he was wrong. During World War I (1914-1918), planes were used in the newest form of combat, as aerial dogfights became commonplace in European skies. After the war, the airplane continued to make the world a smaller place when, during the twenties and thirties, passenger flights became quite a common method of travel for the wealthiest tourists.

The Wright Brothers concentrated

The Wright brothers' military flyer of 1909. In World War I, airplanes would be used as weapons. The Wright brothers had thought this impossible in 1903, imagining they had invented something that would prevent wars.

Le Petit Journal

L'AÉROPLANE DE WILBUR WRIGHT EN PLEIN VOL

Illustration in a French magazine of a flying exhibition by Wilbur Wright. It was a Frenchman, Louis Bleriot, who first flew across the English Channel in 1909.

their efforts on developing the airplane because they believed that the automobile was merely a contraption of curiosity. They believed that it would certainly never take the place of the horse and buggy or the brothers' first interest, the bicycle. It is most fortunate for the world of aviation that the brothers chose to study aeronautics, while others pursued the idea of developing an automobile for middle-class America.

The Auto Industry

Contrary to the Wright Brothers' prediction, the automobile did replace the horse and buggy and bicycle early in the twentieth century. Karl Benz had produced the first gasoline-powered motorcar in Germany in 1885. As word and photographs of these "horseless European vehicles" or "carriages," appeared in the United States, just about every local mechanical genius began building one. But most of these were isolated people across the country making a single machine for personal use.

The first motorcar to actually appear in the United States was an electric version. Reports and pictures appeared in newspapers in Chicago in September 1892. In 1897, the Renault brothers of Paris perfected a three-speed transmission; the same year Oldsmobile made its debut in the United States. Ransom Eli Olds had built his first gasoline-powered car the year before. In 1898, Alexander Winton sold the first auto powered by an internal combustion engine in the United States. Pierce-Arrow began producing cars in 1901, and by 1903, both the Ford and Buick motor companies were established.

In 1900, sixty-one licensed automobile manufacturers existed in the United States; twelve of these were large companies. By 1908, that number would grow to 253 manufacturers, with fifty-two producing cars in large numbers. Many other companies that were licensed to produce autos never got past the planning stage, while others failed because of faulty business practices. Those who did succeed ran smooth productions, governing their businesses well and reinvesting their profits.

Early cars were skeletal frames on large, spoked wheels, with high, open seats, devoid of windshields and doors. Steering sticks instead of wheels jutted from the floorboards. The first automobile with a steering wheel was the Maxwell, designed in 1904. Most early autos were loud and smelly vehicles, seen as toys of the mechanically inclined and luxuries only of the well-to-do.

Packard and Cadillac opened for business in 1902; using new tables of metal stress, they figured out how many pounds of pressure metals of various thicknesses could withstand. They added springs to their autos in order to ensure some comfort as motorists drove down the bumpy cobblestone streets.

Auto Mania

Americans began to recognize that their contribution to the automobile would be one of adaptation, not invention. They would make the car available to the average family.

Auto fever took America by storm in 1903 after three transcontinental crossings that summer demonstrated that automobiles could withstand hard use on primitive roads in bad weather. The first crossing was made by Dr. H. Nelson Jackson, a Burlington, Vermont, physician, and his chauffeur, Sewall K. Crocker, who traveled, in a Winton, from San Francisco to New York City in sixty-three days. A Packard driven by Tom Fetch traveled the same distance in fifty-three days in order to promote the car for its manufacturers. Shortly thereafter, Eugene Hammond and L. L. Whitman drove

A Ford 999 racing in 1902 at Grosse Pointe, Michigan, from a painting by H. Charles McBarron. Farmers complained that speeding autos scared their livestock, but racing helped speed the advance of auto technology.

a curved-dash Oldsmobile from California to Detroit.

The publicity from these tours enhanced the reputation of all three manufacturers. The auto's growing popularity concerned horse and buggy traders and raised the ire of farmers because speeding autos were scaring their livestock. But, despite these concerns, Olds sales rose to four thousand cars in 1903.

As autos became popular, many Americans followed the trans-continental trend, and, by 1904, several thousand people were taking cross-country driving vacations. The American Automobile Association organized a major tour from New York to the St. Louis Exposition between July 25 and August 10, 1904. Fifty-nine cars completed the trip.

In addition to touring, many Americans became excited by the notion of auto racing. According to auto historian James J. Flink, the races "met with wide public disapproval. They were considered dangerous exhibitions, unwarranted because their importance for the development of a reliable family car seemed remote. . . . Public opinion notwith-standing, contests stressing speed undoubtedly did contribute much to automotive technology." Catching the car fever, audiences flocked to auto shows during the first half of the decade. By 1905, the New York Show at Madison Square Garden was considered the nation's leading indus-trial exhibition.

From Luxuries to Lifesavers

Then, suddenly, tragedy made the auto's reliability and usefulness leg-endary. On April 18, 1906, a severe earthquake shook San Francisco. Fires broke out as gas stoves blew, electric wires were damaged, and gas lamps exploded. The city's water supply was cut off when water mains broke, leav-ing firefighters helpless. Fires spread unchecked for three days. About 700 people died and more than 300,000 lost their homes before the massive fires could be controlled.

Motor trucks were pressed into service to bring needed supplies to the community, and more than two hundred private autos were used to transport volunteers, victims, and equipment. Breakdowns were infre-quent. While horses were dropping from heat exhaustion, autos contin-ued to run. Tires exploded from the heat of the pavement, yet the autos continued for days on their wheel rims. About fifteen thousand gallons of fuel donated by the Standard Oil Company were consumed. The *San Francisco Chronicle* heralded the auto-mobile as indispensable in saving parts

Maxwell was one of the first auto companies to replace the steering stick with a wheel. With the coming of the automobile, wealthier women found a new freedom from the home.

Automobiles proved their worth in the aftermath of the 1906 San Francisco earthquake, when fire destroyed much of the city. Horses finally collapsed from heat and exhaustion, but trucks continued to carry supplies and equipment.

of the city from the fire. When it was all over, the earthquake in San Francisco was seen as the turning point for the automobile's acceptance as a means of family transportation.

An Affordable Automobile

Auto clubs began springing up all over the country and demand grew for a car with a sticker price of $700 to $900. Makers of Oldsmobiles and Packards managed to make them more affordable as they continued to produce their cars one car at a time. Nevertheless, cheaper cars were in demand in tremendous quantities. Factories couldn't keep up with demands for parts.

On November 20, 1901 the Henry Ford Company opened with a plan to concentrate on race cars, but by June 16, 1903, Ford had left this company to found the Ford Motor Company. Although Ford had origi-

nally designed cars for the well-to-do, he came to believe that all people should be able to own a car. Later in the decade, he pioneered the use of assembly-line methods to develop and mass-produce the Model T. Ford could sell these cars at a price the average person could afford because of the savings of time and money he

Henry Ford was the first to realize that cars could be mass-produced at a price many could afford. He introduced assembly-line methods and modern principles of scientific management into his plants, developing this Model T in 1908, probably the most famous auto of all time.

achieved from using the assembly-line techniques he had invented.

Ford's fortunes increased further when he incorporated some of Frederick Taylor's principles of scien-

A New York City electric streetcar in the early 1900s. Improvements in public transportation kept pace with the automobile inventions of the decade. The railways expanded, too, adding faster routes and luxuries to tempt passengers away from the automobile.

tific management into his plants. He continued to reinvest his money in his company, and on January 1, 1910 he opened an elaborately equipped, sixty-acre automobile manufacturing plant in Highland Park, a suburb of Detroit, Michigan.

Public Transportation Improves

While an affordable automobile was being developed for private owners, automotive inventions quickly improved public transportation. On January 2, 1900, the first electric bus with seats for eight passengers and a five-cent fare rolled down Fifth Avenue in New York. On January 6 of the same year, New York's governor contracted for the New York subway

to be built by John B. McDonald. The first American subway had been built in Boston in 1897, but plans for the New York subway would make it the largest in the world. The first sections of this electrically powered system were opened in 1904.

Railroads added routes and passenger cars to compete against the auto. In 1902, the Pennsylvania Railroad was granted a franchise to build tunnels under the East River in New York City. Until then, travelers were required to leave the trains and take ferries across the river. These tunnels were all completed in 1909.

The Death of Commercial Sailing Ships

Large shipping concerns were changing their method of fueling to take advantage of technological advances during the first decade of the twentieth century. By the turn of the century, merchants saw undeniable signs that the days of commercial sailing ships were numbered. Steam-driven ships carried more cargo and traveled faster and further with less need for maintenance. Harbors became littered with the stripped remains of sailing vessels as tradesmen and manufacturers looked to steamships for cargo transport. The Panama Canal's opening in 1914 would be seen as the ultimate death of sailing ships, since fuel-powered vessels were able to make the passage from the Atlantic to the Pacific with fewer stops, thereby making the voyage less expensive.

Alternative sources of power for these ships were also being developed. The steam turbine, developed in 1894 by Charles A. Parsons, an Irish engineer, was a tremendous improvement over the steam engine. The turbine was smaller and more efficient, needed less maintenance, and hardly vibrated when running. It quickly gained acceptance as tradesmen looked to improve their transportation methods. While Parsons was developing his steam turbine, Rudolf Diesel, a German mechanical engineer, was perfecting his diesel engine, which used heavy oil as fuel. It used less fuel and took up less room than the turbine, but would not come into use until the next decade.

By 1904, the Cunard cruise line had ordered two ships powered by steam turbines. They were designed to carry 38,000 tons of cargo and passengers apiece. Each ship was powered by four turbines turning four propellers and was capable of sailing at over twenty-five knots. These huge vessels, launched in 1906, were named the *Mauretania* and the *Lusitania*. Each carried over twenty-five hundred passengers in reasonable comfort, and ushered in the era of luxury ocean-liner travel. Mobility increased dramatically as many Americans and Europeans made the transatlantic crossing in these floating palaces.

Some ships were designed for a specific purpose. The *U.S.S. Gluckauf*, built in Great Britain in 1886, was designed to carry oil. Other ships were built specifically for mineral ores such as copper and iron, or grain, or fruit. Each was built with at least four cargo holds and some with as many as six. Each ship was up to six hundred feet long. They were, in effect, giant steel boxes steaming across the waters. In 1900, almost thirty million tons of merchandise and raw materials were transported by steamship throughout the world. By 1910, over forty-one million tons of goods would be carried in steamship holds.

Inventions Shrink the World

Americans discovered that new transportation and communication methods made their world shrink. Where once it had taken months to cross the country by wagon train, the railroad made it possible to make the trip in just a few days. A trip from one state to another was suddenly possible because of the advent of the automobile. And an ocean voyage to Europe took days rather than weeks

because the steamship cut the traveling time significantly.

Small wonder, then, that U.S. manufacturers and producers began to look upon the entire world as their marketplace. But, to enter that world marketplace, the United States government would also have to become politically involved in international troubles. This would in turn lead to problems at home because many Americans wanted to stay out of foreign affairs.

The Mauretania *launched the era of the ocean liner, in 1906, bringing luxury transatlantic travel. But other giant steamships were individually designed to carry a variety of different cargoes, such as oil, ore, fruit, and grain.*

CHAPTER 7
The Arts Mirror Society's Problems

The first decade of this century saw an increase in the demand for easy reading material and light entertainment. But more serious international and regional artists also found an American audience and passed to it socially significant messages. A new spirit of realism crept into literature, painting, and sculpture.

The ruling elders in the field of literature included Mark Twain, Henry James, and William Dean Howells. All three were firmly established by 1900. During the early 1900s, Twain published mainly short works of fiction and pronouncements upon public events in magazines, but his popularity never waned and his earlier, longer works continued to be read extensively. For James, this decade would be one of his most prolific, since between 1900 and 1904 he wrote *The Wings of the Dove, The Ambassadors,* and *The Golden Bowl.* He also wrote short stories, a biography, and another novel over the same period. James's intellectual novels contrasted naive and crass Americans with rich, cultured, educated Europeans. While Twain interspersed humor into his social commentaries, James and Howells painted dismal and painful pictures of humanity's problems in their writings. Howells attacked American sentimentality and romanticism in fiction, realistically depicting the world through his novels.

Newer writers also came to the fore. Theodore Dreiser wrote *Sister Carrie* in 1900, which was suppressed because of its frank depiction of illicit love. In fact, following rejection by several other publishers and a great deal of reluctance, the publisher issued the book in a small edition without a name on the cover. Willa Cather was a young novelist who would write some of her best work early in this century. During this decade, she worked on the staff of *McClure's* magazine, while she wrote her first novel, *Alexander's Bridge,* which was published in 1912.

Popular, easy-to-read books at the turn of the century included the writer (not the statesman) Winston Churchill's *Richard Carvel* and Helen Keller's autobiography. *Rebecca of Sunnybrook Farm,* by Kate Douglas Wiggin, was one of the most popular books of 1903. The public's taste for easy reading made romanticism hard to avoid. Even Jack London lapsed into the romantic with

(Right) Author Jack London had his first success with The Call of the Wild, *a novel that romanticized the primitive and mystical. Along with adventure stories, he also wrote a political novel,* The Iron Heel, *and an autobiographical story,* John Barleycorn.

Helen Keller. (1880-1968)

Helen Keller became blind and deaf as the result of an illness she suffered before she was two years old. Yet her life is a testament to what can be accomplished by a determined spirit.

As a young child, Keller lived in a silent world. Her family was unable to communicate with her, although she appeared bright, and she developed into a willful and wild child.

Keller's father spoke to Dr. Alexander Graham Bell about his daughter, and he recommended that the Kellers contact the Perkins Institute for the Blind in Boston. When Keller was seven, the Perkins Institute sent Anne Sullivan to teach her to speak using the finger alphabet, to read Braille, and to write. She set limits on Keller's behavior and encouraged her to learn about the world. She even taught her how to talk.

Keller entered Radcliffe in 1900 with Sullivan at her side to spell out lectures. She was expected to do the same amount of work as all the other students. Keller graduated with honors.

She then devoted her life to teaching people about the blind. After her graduation, Keller became active with the American Foundation for the Blind and the American Foundation for Overseas Blind. She urged the U.S. government to print books for the blind and raised money for these activities.

But without Miss Sullivan's dedication and guidance, it would have been impossible for Keller to achieve success. While Keller was a student at Radcliffe, her autobiography was published in *Ladies Home Journal*. Of Miss Sullivan, she wrote, "Had it not been for her devotion, adaptability and willingness to give up every individual pleasure, we should long ago have found it necessary to retire to complete isolation."

In 1902, this autobiography was published as a book called *The Story of My Life*. Before the decade was over, Keller would go on to publish *Optimism, The World I Live In* and *Song of the Stone Wall*. She would publish seven more books before her death in 1968, and they would be published in more than fifty languages.

Not only did Keller become a spokesperson for the disabled, she became an advocate of women's rights, child welfare, and labor reform. She began to write about these subjects. She marched in "Votes for Women" parades and later lectured on labor reform and the rights of the working class. Keller's political views received a lukewarm reception, and magazine editors, who had eagerly accepted past articles, began to reject her work based on her politics rather than its quality.

In 1905, Sullivan married John Macy, a Socialist and writer who influenced Keller to join the Socialist party. Money became a problem for Keller. She lived with Sullivan and Macy, who had their own financial difficulties. Nevertheless, Keller turned down a $5,000-a-year pension offered to her by an admiring Andrew Carnegie.

Keller's life received much publicity because it was so unusual for a child with handicaps to receive the amount of education that she had at that time. Of her curiosity and intellect she wrote, "My hands felt every motion and in this way I learned to know many things." Of her deafness and blindness, Keller recalled, "Gradually I got used to the silence and darkness that surrounded me and forgot that it had ever been any different."

his 1903 novel *The Call of the Wild*, followed by *Sea Wolf* in 1904. In his work, London, philosophically a left-wing Socialist and social critic, glorifies the primitive, mystical side of life.

Poetry and Portrayals

Although Paul Laurence Dunbar, an Ohio-born poet and novelist, would never be considered by critics to be one of the country's major writers, his work left an impression of black America for future generations. Writing about the lives, customs, and language of black America in the early 1900s,

Dunbar captured the dignity and humor of southern blacks in the face of hardship, portraying black life realistically and honestly. His first book, *The Sport of the Gods*, was published in 1902. His most famous poems, written in black dialect, include "When Malindy Sings" and "When De Co'n Pone's Hot."

William Carlos Williams created

> *"In the face of the facts that modern man lives more wretchedly than the cave-man, and that his producing power is a thousand times greater that that of the cave-man, no other conclusion is possible than that capitalist class has...criminally and selfishly mismanaged."*
>
> Jack London, *The Iron Heel*, 1906

Paul Laurence Dunbar. (1872-1906)

Paul Laurence Dunbar was an African-American novelist and poet who portrayed black life realistically and honestly. Dunbar's father had escaped from slavery in Kentucky before the Civil War and settled in Dayton, Ohio, before Paul was born on June 27, 1872.

Education was always important to the family. Dunbar's mother had gone to night school and taught him to read and write before he entered first grade. Dunbar's father died when he was eight, so Paul and his brothers went to work as street lighters to help make ends meet. There was never a question about whether the boys would finish school.

In high school, Dunbar and his brothers attended their first minstrel show. Dunbar quickly realized that the show was a parody of African-Americans, making them appear shiftless, lazy, and stupid. He believed he could create stronger portrayals of his people and began to write with this in mind. Throughout high school, he had poems published in the *Dayton Herald*, but was turned down for a job as a reporter because he was black.

Dunbar published the *Tattler*, a black newspaper that was printed by the Wright brothers, whom he had befriended in eighth grade. Meanwhile, he tried to find work. The only job he could obtain was as elevator operator for $4 a week. In 1893, Dunbar went to join his brothers in Chicago.

In 1893, his first book of poetry, *Oak and Ivory*, was published privately, followed by *Majors and Minors* in 1895. Many praised his dialect poems, while others, including his wife, Alice Moore, criticized them. "I didn't start as a dialect poet," he confided in a friend. "I simply came to the conclusion that I could write it as well, if not better than anyone else I know. And that by doing so, I should gain a hearing. I gained a hearing and now they don't want me to write anything but dialect."

Dunbar wrote several novels between 1896 and 1902, but they were never as popular as his poems.

a stir when he published *Poems* in 1909. The poems defied traditional conventions and were written for the average American rather than for the intellectual elite. Ezra Pound published *Personae* and *Exultations* that same year. These works represented a short-lived poetic movement called imagery, in which poets used common language to describe everyday objects and sights to convey their messages. Their poetry was in the way they used metaphor and rhythm.

Sentimental and Serious Theater

Many plays of the first decade reflected the American public's interest in entertainment, rather than a serious message. "The greatest actress in the world," Sarah Bernhardt, appeared on stage in 1900 in *Camille*, a melodramatic story of love and death. Richard Mansfield appeared in *Dr. Jekyll and Mr. Hyde*. Ethel Barrymore, of the Barrymore acting clan, starred in *Captain Jinks of the Horse Marines* and the Four Cohans, known as "the favorite family of funrakers," played in *The Governor's Son*, written by George M. Cohan. But the most popular play of the decade was the child's fantasy *Peter Pan*, starring Maude Adams. These plays were a direct contrast to the more serious social dramas. They offered audiences a lighthearted escape through romance and sentimentality.

Theater also reflected the realism that seemed to be influencing literature. Although *Peter Pan* and other lighter fare were popular, serious playwrights also left their mark dur-

ing this decade. George Bernard Shaw's plays were produced for the first time between 1905 and 1906. Full of symbolism and promoting naturalism, the Irish playwright portrayed humanity's plight with an irreverent wit.

Plays dealt with serious social and personal problems, too. Openly dealing with the issue of prostitution, Shaw's *Mrs. Warren's Profession* was closed for immorality by police in New York. Critics denounced it as

Maude Adams was a popular actress who often portrayed boys on the stage. Many of her greatest successes were roles in J. M. Barrie's plays, as here in Peter Pan.

"revolting in theme" and "a pervading poison." In 1907, Henrik Ibsen's *A Doll's House* was brought to New York. The play shocked audiences by questioning a woman's role in life. The heroine continually disputes her husband's domination and finally leaves him.

William Vaughn Moody's serious social dramas were brought to the stage in *The Great Divide* in 1906 and *The Faith Healer* in 1909. Israel Zangwill's *The Melting Pot* portrayed Jewish immigrant life and was produced in 1908. All of these plays gave American audiences a strong dose of reality, forcing the public to recognize and respond to the social injustices around them.

Artistic Impressions

In contrast to serious theater, the visual arts contained relatively little social comment during this period. Most of the ferment in the world of art took the form of a revolt against the traditional and formal. Although the romantic influence was at its height, the turn of the century signaled a turning point for the international art world. The work of the romantics was rapidly giving way to impressionism.

The impressionists worked to capture a single moment's impression of light and color on the eye. Claude Monet, a founder of this school of painting, would set up an easel and paint the same scene over and over, capturing each subtle change in light. The American portrait painter, James McNeill Whistler, was influenced by impressionism and carefully arranged his compositions to show the play of light on all the details.

Auguste Renoir and Edgar Degas, two European artists who painted scenes of dancing and revelry filled with women and children, were both influenced by Monet. Degas went so far as to attempt to capture a moment with quick brush strokes to create the illusion of people and animals in motion. His strokes were so swift, broad, and sure that, up close, a cat could appear as just two or three simple streaks of color. When the impressionists first exhibited their works, the public was dismayed by the lack of detail, and their work was only gradually accepted.

Emotions and Expressionism in Art

Other European painters during this time were captivated by the Dutch post-impressionist Vincent Van Gogh and the French painter Paul Cézanne's works. They began to distort objects in their own paintings until the objects could hardly be recognized. Other painters, called expressionists, were represented by Paul Gauguin and Edvard Munch. They used swirling patterns of flat color and simplified details to create overall patterns in their work and thus capture the subject's overpowering emotion.

One emerging painter in the early 1900s would later become one of the most famous artists of the entire twentieth century. Born in Spain, Pablo Picasso responded to changing conditions, moods, and challenges with an intense sensitivity. His art challenged the observer's traditional view of life by exploring the fantastic and the imaginative, thus hoping to arouse the subconscious

"The real American has not yet arrived. He is only in the crucible, I tell you — he will be the fusion of all the races, the coming superman."

Israel Zangwill, *The Melting Pot*, 1908

Guitar was one of Picasso's early cubist paintings. Cubism portrays objects in basic shapes from several different angles at once. American painters followed a different path in this decade. Some chose to portray realistic city scenes in a variety of styles, while others captured the spirit of the landscape and the Wild West.

influences on the lives of his audience. During the first five years of this decade, Picasso painted works that came to be grouped together into his blue period. He focused on themes of loneliness and despair, painting mostly in shades of blue. From 1904 to 1906, he painted images using warmer colors to depict warmer moods and subjects.

In 1907, while living in France, Picasso painted the first of his works in a style that would become the most influential movement in the history of modern art — cubism. Cubism is the portrayal of an object or person in basic geometric shapes and signs, demonstrating several different viewpoints of the object at once. Elements in cubist works are often overlapped and reorganized into simple, repetitive forms. Cubism forced artists to think in terms of multiple dimensions in space.

Americans in Art

American achievement was still small in the arts, and many great artists looked across the ocean to Europe and European artists to feed and polish their art. Like many American painters, John Singer Sargent lived and worked in Paris. Sargent would be remembered for his portraits of the noble and famous of the decade. One writer describes the impact of his work: "His very name whispers of the gilt frames, plush draperies, chandeliers, fringed bellpulls, spats, bowler hats, and potted palms that furnished the Victorian and Edwardian ages." But long before the end of his life, he would tire of the formal portraits that had made his fame and fortune and devote himself to murals and watercolors.

Other American artists, too, turned

away from formal portrait painting and sought other ways to express themselves and explore the meaning of their time. These painters included John Sloan, William Glackens, Maurice Prendergast, George Luks, Arthur B. Davies, Charles Hawthorne, Robert Henri, and Everett Shinn. They remained in their homeland and left an illustrated history of American life with their realistic paintings of city lifestyles. Called "The Eight" because they formed a small artists' colony in Greenwich Village, New York, these painters often exhibited their work together. Collectively, their art soon came to be known as the Ash Can School because of their realistic portrayals of the city slums and back alleys.

John Sloan and William Glackens, who were originally reporter-artists and painted for the city's newspapers, made rapid sketches to tell a story. George Luks painted New York's East Side immigrants. Maurice Prendergast lived in Philadelphia, but on his visits to Greenwich Village, he painted cityscapes with broad strokes of watercolor to create flat, simplified forms. Prendergast gave each element in a painting equal attention to create overall patterns of movement and color on his canvases.

Robert Henri and his wife, Marjorie Organ, worked with swift brush strokes and never used background because it distracted from the main figures of their work. Charles Hawthorne started a summer school in Provincetown, Massachusetts, that later became an artists' colony.

Another member of the Ash Can School was George Bellows. Originally a boxer and professional baseball player, Bellows painted sports figures in action.

Capturing America's Landscape

Other painters also produced images that would document America's rapidly changing culture. Winslow Homer is remembered for his paintings

This political cartoon by George Luks shows an octopus representing monopolistic business engulfing a city with its tentacles. Luks was one of a group of painters known as the "Ash Can School" because they realistically illustrated city slum scenes.

Winslow Homer painted realistic landscapes that captured the spirit of the great outdoors. They contrasted with the paintings of the impressionist and expressionist movements that were popular in Europe at this time.

of Maine's coastline and the wilderness of the northwoods. Thomas Eakins was both a painter and a photographer, whose work stood out because of its distinctive and significant new sports scenes and African-American themes. The brutal realism of the photographs he had taken in medical schools were so gruesome they were censored.

These realistic paintings were in stark contrast to Europe's strong romantic movement, where pictures possessed hazy, dreamlike qualities. One of the greatest American romantic painters was Albert Pinkham Ryder. This fisherman's son from New Bedford, Massachusetts, trained in Paris, then returned to the United States, where he painted landscapes, seascapes, and scenes from myth, legend, and the works of William Shakespeare.

The Old West was also captured by a few painters who had escaped the cities for the romance of open spaces. These painters loved the wild landscapes and lifestyles of the settlers, the country's last pioneers in the West. They captured this spirit in their work. Frederic Remington, a writer, illustrated his works with action-filled paintings and drawings of cattle drives and storms in the West. His works were characterized by the vivid use of color and broad brush strokes. Remington wrote and illustrated a children's book, *The Way of the Indian,* in 1908. Later in his career, he turned to sculpture to capture in three-dimensional form the action he had formerly reproduced on the flat surface of a canvas.

Edwin Cyrus Dallin, an American sculptor who studied in Paris, was influenced there by an international tour of Buffalo Bill's Wild West Show. He used the American Indian way of life as his theme for realistic and dramatic works. His work, *The*

Frederic Remington immortalized the western frontier, at first with colorful, action-packed paintings, and later in three-dimensional form with sculptures like this Bronco-buster. *He was a friend of Owen Wister, whose novel* The Virginian *was a model for numerous westerns of the future.*

(Below) "Gibson Girls," designed by Charles Dana Gibson, appeared as sketches in 1899 and then figured on magazine covers. Elegantly dressed, they enjoyed expensive leisure pursuits and a freedom that few women actually had in that decade. Their appearance became the ideal to which millions of American women aspired.

Appeal to the Great Spirit, is now displayed at the Boston Museum of Fine Arts.

As production and printing tech-niques for magazines and newspapers improved, advertising illustrators gained a wider audience. Charles Dana Gibson would leave his mark with the elegant "Gibson Girl" magazine covers he illustrated for *McCalls* and *Ladies Home Journal.* For many in his audience, the "Gibson Girl" represented a limited freedom from middle-class mores, since she drove cars, played tennis, rode horses, and even, it was whispered, smoked cigarettes and drank whiskey.

Photography — Amateur and Professional

George Eastman developed the lightweight, easy-to-use Kodak box camera in 1888. By 1900, amateurs were snapping photos and creating photo journals to record everyday life for the first time in history. The camera used a roll of gelatin-coated film that could record a hundred round photographs. Once the roll had been shot, the film and camera were sent to one of Eastman's processing labs. Prints were developed and the reloaded camera was sent back to the customer. Kodak's slogan was "You Press the Button, We Do the Rest." Until that time, photography had been practiced only by skilled people who could afford the complicated equipment and developing solutions. Now almost anyone could take a picture.

The impact of amateur photography on professionals was that the professionals began to develop their photography into a creative art, just like painting and drawing. Some professionals used special printing techniques and paper to give their prints the look of paintings. Some even touched up their images with paint.

The easy-to-use Kodak box camera allowed millions to record everyday life. As it became easier for amateurs to take photographs, professionals turned their pictures into art by careful lighting and composition, and the use of special printing techniques.

One group of photographers, called photo-secessionists, organized in 1902, when Alfred Stieglitz and Edward Steichen set up photo exhibits around the United States to promote photography as an art form. These photo artists stressed the elements of lighting and composition in their work. Describing his artistic goals, Stieglitz once said, "I told Miss [Georgia] O'Keeffe I wanted a series of photographs which when seen. . . exclaim 'Music! Music! Man, why that's music!'"

Public Art

Sculpture was being created to decorate America's city parks and avenues. Citizens took pride in their own history. Augustus Saint-Gaudens, George Grey Barnard, Daniel Chester French, and Lorado Taft carved

famous statesmen and generals to stand guard over public grounds across America.

Building styles displayed the contemporary tastes for the romantic, yet functional. Reflecting the country's prosperity and contentment, architectural styling seemed light and easy. The Woolworth Building in New York, which was designed during this decade and would be opened in 1913, was just one example. The building contains long, straight lines and displays elegance with graceful but clean angles.

Frank Lloyd Wright was just becoming known, with his low and straight-lined home designs, said to aesthetically combine form and function. Called "prairie homes," Wright's architecture attracted attention because it was designed to fit in with surrounding landscapes. He sometimes incorporated the local tim-

Alfred Stieglitz. (1864-1946)

Although he is remembered primarily as a photographer, Alfred Stieglitz was also a painter, sculptor, and organizer of some of the most radical artists' exhibits of the twentieth century. An engineering student in Europe in 1881, he turned to photography and, by 1890, was championing photography as a fine art. He was a self-styled loner and rebel, who responded to amateur photography by organizing, along with Edward Steichen, the photo-secessionist movement. The movement aimed to bring photography into the realm of art and to separate it from the snapshots created by amateur shutterbugs. The photo-seccessionist photographers used composition and lighting to create some of the moods and themes found in contemporary paintings.

In 1905, Stieglitz opened his Gallery 291, at 291 Fifth Avenue, in New York City, where he exhibited his and Steichen's work. In 1908, he exhibited the work of Henri Matisse and went on to bring more of Europe's most radical artists to America. Over the next few years, he exhibited the works of Pablo Picasso, French primitive painter Henri Rousseau, and cubist painter Georges Braque.

Although Stieglitz was an artist caught up in the avant garde art world of New York City, he also loved the peace of domestic life, which he found with his family in Lake George, New York. Stieglitz married twice, and his second wife was painter Georgia O'Keeffe.

Through both marriages and through his career as gallery owner, he continued to produce the photographic masterpieces for which he is remembered. In a letter, he described himself as a "photographic vagabond here, there and everywhere."

ber and rock found around the home as part of the overall design. Often, the first floor of a Wright home was one large room. Windows tended to be wide. The simple lines were reminiscent of earlier Shaker designs. Mission-style furniture, which Wright designed for his prairie homes, was also simple. Spindles and legs were often straight, flat pieces of mahogany and oak. One example of a Wright prairie home, the Willets House, was built in 1902, and can still be seen in Highland Park, Illinois.

Wright also began building large wood and concrete office buildings, churches, and temples during the first decade of the 1900s. The Unity Church in Oak Park, Illinois, was built in 1903. With its poured concrete masses and skylighted interior, it was quite controversial at the time.

He completed the Larkin Building in Buffalo in 1904, which contained a courtyard with skylights in its center. This building had a strong influence over architecture in the United States and Europe in its day.

More skyscrapers were appearing and the country's skyline soon reflected the shape of these newest works of architectural art. With an eye toward function, Daniel E. Burnham designed the building on record as America's first skyscraper, the Flatiron building in New York. The 180-foot-tall building was constructed in 1902 and 1903.

New York City, with its high land prices and crowded streets, provided a natural home for the skyscraper. In 1908, Ernest Flagg designed and built the seven-hundred-foot, forty-seven-story Singer Building. That same year, Metropolitan Life Tower, designed by Napoleon Le Brun, added its seven-hundred-foot silhouette to the city's skyline.

Using a classic renaissance style, New York's Pierpont Morgan Library, on the East Side, was built during this decade. Using similar lines, but a more ornate design to accommodate its low structure, the Pennsylvania Station in New York City was designed in 1906 and completed in 1910.

The Flatiron building in New York, completed in 1903, was one of America's first skyscrapers. Many more would appear in the next few years, a result of high land prices and crowded cities.

Isadora Duncan. (1878-1927)

Isadora Duncan was born in San Francisco, the fourth child of John and Mary Duncan. Her father deserted the family before Isadora's birth, and she grew up in poverty. But Isadora always seemed to know she would reap fame through dance. When she was little more than six years old, her mother discovered Isadora teaching babies to gracefully wave their arms. She told her mother this was a dance school.

In 1896, Duncan moved with her mother to Chicago, where she danced in roof gardens. Her audience most often comprised society ladies, who paid her to entertain at social events. Although she received little pay, Duncan found fulfillment in these dances she created herself. Because they interpreted music, they were freeform and rarely repeated.

Rebelling against the classical forms of dance, by 1898, Duncan had developed a series of dances that displayed creativity, imagination, and grace through free-flowing movement and pantomime. She usually danced barefoot to the music of Beethoven, Chopin, and Gluck.

Her audiences loved her in Europe, but Duncan found less acceptance in the United States. Although she became a "pet of society," many found her dancing shocking or ridiculous, since Duncan wore filmy dresses that exposed her arms and legs. She established schools for children in France, Germany, and Russia, but they were unable to gain much of a following because Duncan's expressive techniques were everchanging.

In 1907, Duncan danced at the Metropolitan Opera House in New York City. The critics treated her with respect, but when Duncan proclaimed her theories from the stage — theories on dance of the future, the proper training of children, on her hopes for a school in America, and on love — many responded critically because her liberal views were hard to accept.

In her autobiography, Duncan said, "My Art is just an effort to express the truth of my Being in gesture and movement. . . . Before the public which has thronged my representations I have had no hesitations, I have given them the most secret impulses of my soul. From the first I have only danced my life. As a child I danced the spontaneous joy of growing things. As an adolescent, I danced with joy turning into apprehension of the pitiless brutality and crushing progress of life."

"To Live in the Scene . . ."

Expressionism also influenced dance during this decade. American Isadora Duncan began performing her expressive interpretation of music in 1903. Although she was extremely successful in Europe, American audiences didn't really accept her until 1908. She was simply too radical for conservative America. Duncan performed her free-form interpretative dance in short tunics that exposed her arms and legs at a time when women were shamed if they exposed a bit of ankle below their skirts.

It is likely that Duncan expressed best the artistic mood of the times when she described her goals for dance. She said, "This is what we are trying to accomplish, to blend together a poem, a melody and a dance, so that you will not listen to music, see the dance or hear the poem, but will live in the scene and the thought that all are expressing."

It seemed that Americans caught up in the expressive movement were eager to rid themselves of past traditions. With both hands they grasped toward the excitement of change.

"Dance is a religion and should have its worshipers."

Isadora Duncan, 1900

CHAPTER 8
"Carry a Big Stick:" The United States Intervenes Abroad

By the turn of the twentieth century, improvements in transportation made the world seem a smaller place. The growth of European, and later, American, industry from the mid-1700s through the 1800s created a worldwide system of markets. This led, at the end of the 1800s, to a rise in European imperialism as many nations, including Belgium, France, Germany, Great Britain, Italy, and Spain, colonized most of Africa, Southeast Asia, and the South Pacific islands. Of these areas, only Japan and Siam (now Thailand) remained independent. China was under the influence of European nations. While other countries around the world underwent colonization, the Latin American countries, through a series of wars of liberation, gained freedom from European domination.

Imperialism and Anti-imperialism

Despite the desire of many in the United States to remain neutral, the country could no longer remain isolated in the new world arena. Arguments brewed within the nation as imperialists supported the idea of colonizing lands to protect the new capitalism. Advocates of imperialism included Secretary of State John Hay,

Theodore Roosevelt, and Senator Henry Cabot Lodge, who saw acquisition of foreign lands as an opportunity to extend commerce into the Orient. They reflected the general opinion of merchants and business owners, who believed that the increase in manufacturing capacity created by new technologies made foreign outlets absolutely necessary to United States' commerce. They insisted that foreign acquisition was necessary to expand markets, protect seaways, and supply raw materials needed by American industry. Church and missionary groups proved to be strong allies in the imperialists' camp because they believed that the United States had no choice but to meet the moral responsibilities of creating a better existence for the poor and less fortunate nations thrust upon it in its victories.

Anti-imperialists who spoke out against acquiring the colonies after the Spanish-American War included former President Grover Cleveland, political leader William Jennings Bryan, and Thomas Reed, the Republican Speaker of the House until 1899, who argued that there was no place in a republican form of government for colonial possessions. The United States, they claimed, had no moral right to impose its rule upon people by force.

"Speak softly and carry a big stick, you will go far."

West African proverb, adapted by Theodore Roosevelt

The issue of protection and economic control of foreign lands in America's backyard became increasingly important. As early as 1823, the United States, acting in the spirit of its Monroe Doctrine, moved to "protect" Latin American countries from any attempts to re-establish or expand European colonial rule there. Military and economic intervention safeguarded the many American interests in the region.

After victory in the Mexican War, fought between 1846 and 1848, the United States gained additional territory that included California, Nevada, Utah, and parts of four other states — an odd sort of protection. To further expand its markets, and uncover possible raw materials, the government bought Alaska from Russia in 1867.

Conquest Through Capitalism

President McKinley favored the "Open Door" policy of free trade, where any country was allowed to trade freely with any other. It was hoped that, in this way, the United States could establish its international position through economic imperialism, rather than the military and political imperialism favored by the great European powers.

Hitherto, countries in the world market had operated under a "sphere of influence" policy. This meant that those countries with influence and power over others would grant tariff reductions and import/export courtesies to their allies while making it difficult for others to trade in the international marketplace. For the European nations, this influence and power extended to colonizing by force. The United States wanted to break up the spheres of influence and initiate free trade in all foreign markets. Of special interest to the U.S., apart from Latin America, were the rich lands of Asia and the strategically important Pacific islands of Hawaii and the Philippines.

Central to America's vision of the Open Door policy was the construction of a canal across the Isthmus of Panama to link the eastern ports with the Pacific. The large Caribbean island of Cuba, then under Spanish rule, was an essential element in the equation, too.

Controls on Cuba

Because of the tensions between Spain's military imperialism and America's economic imperialism, military conflict was inevitable. Under McKinley's leadership, the country entered into the Spanish-American War in 1898. The United States had become involved in the war to "liberate" Cuba from Spain and, at the same time, to protect its substantial investments in the plantations, mining, and other business enterprises on the island. The war lasted less than a year, and the Spanish were easily defeated.

Although Cuba did not become a U.S. possession in the negotiations to end the war, the United States did set up a provisional government for the island. And as it did so, Congress proclaimed, "that all people of Cuba are and of right ought to be free and independent." The United States promised to leave the government and control of the island to the people once native rebellions for control

"In disregard of our pledge of freedom and sovereignty to Cuba we are imposing on that island conditions of colonial vassalage."

George Boutwell, at a meeting of the American Anti-Imperialist League

had been pacified. However, America continued to play a leading role in the government of the country for many years.

On June 12, 1901, Cuba accepted the Platt Amendment, agreeing not to accrue debts the island could not meet and never to enter into any agreement that would permit a foreign power to control any part of the island. The island's government also promised to extend hygienic measures that were eliminating some epidemics and diseases. The amendment, intended to be a permanent treaty between the United States and Cuba, gave the United States the power and right to intervene if Cuba's independence, government, or people were threatened from within or without.

American anti-imperialists found the treaty offensive because it gave the United States power over the island. Cuban nationals opposed it because it kept them under the thumb of the U.S. But McKinley convinced the Cubans that this would permit Cuba to market sugar crops to their advantage in the United States. It would encourage a philosophy of reciprocity because as

African-American cavalrymen in Cuba during the Spanish-American War. Theodore Roosevelt came back from the war a national hero. An all-black infantry unit that also served there was greeted in Texas, some years later, with signs proclaiming "No niggers and dogs allowed."

(Far right) Roosevelt, sitting in a giant steam shovel in 1906, examines the digging of the Panama Canal. The idea of a canal linking the Atlantic and Pacific oceans had been around for hundreds of years without the technology necessary to fulfill it.

long as Cuba was protected by the United States, imports from Cuba into the United States incurred a lower tariff, or tax, than imports from other countries.

A New Government in the Philippines

Meanwhile, diplomats and troops were kept busy trying to put an end to an insurrection in the Philippines. In the settlement of the Spanish-American war in 1898, Spain gave over the government of the Philippines to the United States. When the Filipinos learned that instead of coming to liberate them from Spain, Americans had come to the archipelago simply to establish their own rule, they rose in rebellion. The United States regained control of

the islands on March 27, 1901, after three years of harsh warfare that employed sixty thousand troops and led to several thousand American casualties. More than 200,000 Philippine civilians died from privation, disease, and brutality in this guerrilla war.

The United States soon began the task of preparing the islands for self-government. William H. Taft became acting governor of the Philippines on July 4, 1901. He immediately began sending in hundreds of American teachers to serve native schools and encouraged Filipinos to participate in the territorial government. Under Taft's direction, the Filipinos learned all about America's favorite pastime, baseball, along with hygiene and other subjects.

With the teachers and economic aid, many Americans could tell them-

This 1904 cartoon by W. A. Rogers shows Roosevelt with his "big stick" over his shoulder pulling the U.S. Navy around the Caribbean. He is enforcing the Monroe Doctrine, which, Roosevelt proclaimed, allowed military and economic intervention in neighboring countries to safeguard American interests.

selves that they had taken over another country against the wishes of its citizens in order to improve it. But for many in the American government and big businesses, the goal was not so altruistic. The Philippines provided American access to the teeming markets of Asia and the huge, under-developed resources of its countries, which could be developed to fuel America's own industries.

A Man, a Plan, a Canal, Panama

Roosevelt, like many of his predecessors, believed that unlimited growth for U.S. markets could also be acquired by both defining Alaska's boundaries to include strategic ports, and by gaining control of Panama. He dreamed of a canal connecting the Atlantic and Pacific Oceans. This dream had first taken shape for Europeans during the Age of Discovery when the Spanish came to the continent hundreds of years before. Now there was the technology available to fulfill that dream.

Roosevelt planned to take the Isthmus of Panama (then under Colombian control) by force rather than cave in to Colombia's demand for $40 million in payment for the land. But this plan soon became unnecessary. Panamanian leaders planned a revolution, inspired by the promise of money and financed by Philippe Bunau-Varilla, the chief agent of the New Panama Canal Company in the United States. Although Roosevelt and his Secretary of State, John Hay, did not openly encourage the revolution that was scheduled to take place on November 3, 1903, they made it

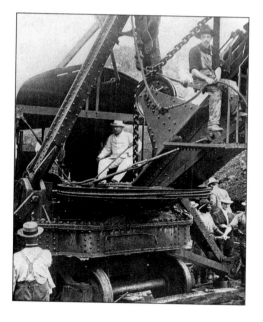

clear to Bunau-Varilla that the United States government would not allow it to fail. The *U.S.S. Nashville* arrived at Colon on the Atlantic side of the isthmus the day before Colombian troops attempted to land to fight the rebels. Under instructions from Washington, the *Nashville's* commander forbade the Colombian troops to march across the isthmus. Additional U.S. vessels followed to protect the Atlantic terminal of the Panama Railroad. The Colombians turned back two days later. By November 5, the rebels controlled the isthmus while the United States protected both coasts.

On November 6, 1903, Roosevelt publicly recognized the new Republic of Panama, and a new canal agreement was signed on November 19. The Hay-Bunau-Varilla Treaty guaranteed Panama independence in exchange for a perpetual lease to a ten mile-wide zone on which the U.S. could build a canal.

Colombians and many Americans

"We have pacified some thousands of the islanders and buried them . . . burned their villages, and turned their widows and orphans out-of-doors . . . subjugated the remaining ten millions by benevolent assimilation, which is the pious new name of the musket; we have acquired property in the three hundred concubines and other slaves of our business partner, the Sultan of Sulu, and hoisted our protecting flag over that swag. And so, by these Providences of God — and the phrase is the government's, not mine — we are a world power."

Mark Twain,
regarding the
Philippine war

were critical of Roosevelt's overt involvement in Panama's revolution. U.S. leaders responded to criticism over their involvement with the argument that they were operating under an older treaty that guaranteed the isthmus would remain neutral. Although Roosevelt's reasons for taking sides during the revolution may appear justified, it created ill-will between Latin American countries and the United States for many years to come.

Construction of the canal, which Roosevelt believed to be his single biggest contribution during his presidency, began in 1904. At first the

project was placed under the control of chief engineer, John F. Stevens. However, by 1907, Roosevelt, impatient at the canal's slow progress, had replaced Stevens with Lieutenant Colonel George Goethals. The canal would finally be opened on August 15, 1914.

Roosevelt threatened military intervention in other disputes, too, most notably in the Alaskan boundary dispute with Canada. Canada had claimed ownership of a large portion of the southeastern border after gold was discovered in the Klondike. Roosevelt, known for his "speak softly and carry a big stick" philosophy, displayed characteristic bravado and announced that there would be dire consequences if the boundaries were changed. The British eventually agreed to help the Canadians and the Americans to settle their dispute — in America's favor.

Promises Not to Interfere . . . Unless

Meanwhile, some European nations had been trying to force several Latin American nations to repay debts owed to them. They had steamed into ports and trained their guns on a number of South American harbors. In December of 1904, Roosevelt made his position clear regarding America's role in the affairs of less developed nations nearby. In his annual message to Congress, the president added what became known as the Roosevelt Corollary to the Monroe Doctrine when he said: "If a nation shows that it knows how to act with reasonable efficiency and decency in social and political matters, if it keeps order and

This cartoon shows President Roosevelt and Uncle Sam in Panama, their way blocked by a mountain representing yellow fever. One of the first obstacles to be dealt with in building the Panama Canal was tropical disease. A similar French project had already failed because of yellow fever's toll on the workforce.

pays its obligations, it need fear no interference from the United States . . . . We must make it evident that we do not intend to permit the Monroe Doctrine to be used by any nation on this continent as a shield to protect it from the consequences of its own misdeeds against foreign nations . . ." In other words, the United States was saying that while neighboring nations should not go looking for trouble with other lands, Europe should not consider any further incursions into America's backyard. The United States would use military force to collect on the debts of Latin American nations for the Europeans, thus assuring that these countries would fall under American, rather than European, control.

Later in the decade, both Roosevelt and Taft engaged in what came to be known as "dollar diplomacy." They encouraged American businesses to invest in areas of the world that were of strategic interest to the United States, especially in the countries of Latin America.

An Umbrella of Unity

Since the 1880s, the United States had recognized the need to organize Pan-American countries under an umbrella of unity. But all attempts had been met with suspicion of American motives. Between 1901 and 1902, a Pan-American Conference was held in Mexico City. Latin American countries expressed their apprehension over American imperialism, especially since Cuba was already under U.S. protection. If anything, their concerns mounted as Roosevelt wielded his "big stick" of military intervention or threatened it in countries of the region, such as Panama, Venezuela, and the Dominican Republic.

In 1906 at a conference in Rio de Janeiro, Latin American countries cited the Platt Amendment, America's role in the revolution in Panama, intervention in the Dominican Republic, and the "promulgation of the Roosevelt Corollary" as reasons to suspect America's motives. Argentina, America's biggest rival to hemispheric leadership, countered with the Drago Doctrine. This doctrine demanded that no military force be used to collect debts. This doctrine directly contradicted the Roosevelt Corollary.

Elihu Root, chair of the U.S. delegation to the conference, agreed to submit the debt collection doctrine, written by a committee of Latin American leaders, to the International Court in the Hague, and kept diplomatic discussion to a minimum. The court refused to accept the doctrine as it was written. Delegates amended it to read that armed force would only be used to collect debts if the debtor refused to arbitrate. Root followed up the conference with a political tour to seven Latin American countries to promote better relations.

This tour succeeded in fostering more open relations at the 1910 Latin American conference in Buenos Aires. All the countries at the conference signed a pact agreeing to arbitrate differences among themselves. Delegates addressed issues of mutual concern, such as developing uniform patents and copyright trademarks; improving communication, health, and sanitation; and increasing student/professor exchanges, helping to encourage a global interchange of commercial and academic sharing.

> *"Chronic wrongdoing, or an impotence which results in a general loosening of the ties of civilized society...may force the United States, however reluctantly, in flagrant cases of such wrongdoing or impotence, to the exercise of an international police power."*
>
> Theodore Roosevelt, address to Congress, 1904

Elihu Root. (1845-1937)

An American lawyer, statesman, and cabinet official under presidents McKinley and Theodore Roosevelt, Root's greatest contributions were as international peace-maker. Of this diplomatic servant, author William Allen White wrote, "Probably the most learned, even erudite, distinguished, and impeccable conservative Republican in the United States, he was the idol of the American bar."

In 1899, President McKinley appointed Root secretary of war. In 1905, President Roosevelt appointed Root secretary of state, and he served in this role until 1909. Before he became a cabinet officer, most of Root's clients were giant corporations. As secretary of state, Root often acted as an emissary between big business owners, such as J. P. Morgan, and the president. In this role, Root was able to help Roosevelt play both sides of the fence between business and reform, so Root's friendships with big businesses were appreciated. During the Panic of 1907, he was responsible for helping Morgan organize a securities trade between the Tennessee Coal and Iron Company and the U.S. Steel Corporation that effectively ended the panic.

As secretary of state, Root was also responsible for organizing the Pacific Coast tour of the U.S. Navy in 1907. The Great White Fleet's tour, nicknamed "battleship diplomacy" by Roosevelt, was so popular that Root received numerous requests to reschedule the tour to include small ports in such countries as Chile and Ecuador.

In 1908, Root and Japanese Ambassador Kogoro Takahira worked out a common policy between the countries' movements on the Pacific Ocean, pledging to "reciprocally . . . respect the territorial possessions belonging to each other." Root also proposed and organized the Central American Peace Conference in 1908.

During Roosevelt's administration, Root served as a U.S. member of the joint commission to settle the Alaskan boundary dispute with Canada. Although Roosevelt considered Root as a potential Republican candidate for president in 1908, he believed Root's friendships with business tycoons might inevitably keep him from higher office.

Roosevelt's Diplomatic Efforts

It appeared that Roosevelt's forceful administration smoothed the way to mutual respect between the U.S. and its neighbors and to protection of nearby shores. His diplomatic skill also led to his involvement in negotiating conflicts elsewhere around the world.

During the early part of the century, the United States and Great Britain watched with growing concern as Russia extended its influence over Manchuria and made advances toward Korea. So, in 1903, with U.S. approval, the British began to form an alliance with Japan. Roosevelt felt that, while Japan could become a threat to the U.S., the greater threat came from Russia. This is why, in 1904, when the Japanese launched an attack against Russia, the United States supported Japan. Rumors spread that if France or Germany went to Russia's aid, Roosevelt and the United States would support Japan.

In fact, Japan did approach the United States for help in making peace with Russia. Russia, itself experiencing internal strife, was also eager to end the war. Roosevelt quickly organized meetings between the two countries to negotiate a peace settlement, and the Treaty of Portsmouth was signed on September 5, 1905. Roosevelt received the Nobel Peace Prize for his role in the negotiations.

After analyzing Japan's strength and obvious desire to obtain territory, the Roosevelt administration wanted to safeguard U.S. interests in the Philippines. Secretary of War Taft was dispatched from Manila to Japan to determine Japan's intentions in the region. Toward the close of July 1905, Taft and Prime Minister Katsura concluded the Taft-Katsura memorandum. This agreement effectively gave Japan control over Korea in exchange for a promise to stay out of the Philippines. The agreement was kept secret from the American people for years because it violated the Open Door policy, which called for equitable trade among nations.

Tense Times with the Japanese

Despite this agreement, tensions between the United States and Japan continued to mount because Japan believed that U.S. intervention in the Russo-Japanese War had cost them territory and money. To add to the tension, Americans along the Pacific Coast were growing increasingly worried about Japanese immigration. They believed that the numbers of unskilled laborers entering the country were harming their own economic stability. In October 1906, San Francisco enacted a local ordinance preventing Asians from attending the city's schools. The Japanese government objected, protesting that an earlier treaty gave their people the same rights to jobs, education, and housing as other immigrants.

Roosevelt, who always leaned toward human rights reform, found the ordinance obnoxious and called California's leaders to the White House to encourage them to repeal the statute. Nationally, public sentiments backed Roosevelt because they believed that Japan's strong resentment could lead to war. Without public support, California's legislators had no choice but to amend the school law to allow Japanese children "of proper age and preparation" into the city's schools.

To avoid further state actions, the United States and Japan reached an agreement in 1907, in which the Japanese government would stop granting Japanese laborers passports to the United States. But Roosevelt feared his intervention would be seen as a sign of military weakness; as a result he launched a world tour of the U.S. Navy's battle fleet, consisting of sixteen battleships and numerous smaller craft. The spectacular tour enabled the fleet to demonstrate its strength to Japan, practice large-scale maneuvers, and publicize the need for larger budget appropriations for the fleet itself in order to protect the

Roosevelt made a reputation for himself as a skillful diplomat, organizing the 1905 peace treaty between Russia and Japan. Here he poses with representatives from both sides. At about the same time, the United States and Japan signed a secret agreement in which Japan promised to stay out of the Philippines in exchange for being allowed to control Korea.

Panama Canal. Japan's response to seeing the fleet in Tokyo harbor was to double efforts to strengthen its

The Great White Fleet steams home in 1909 after a forty-six thousand mile cruise around the world. Its mission was to demonstrate to the world, friends as well as potential enemies, the naval might of the United States.

own fleet. Observing their concern, Secretary Root took this opportunity to secure an agreement in November 1908 with Japanese Ambassador Takahira that provided mutual support for the "Pacific status quo" through a promise not to interfere with each other's possessions, mutual backing of China's independence and boundaries, and mutual support of the Open Door policy.

Despite these gains, tensions between the United States and Japan continued to grow. Some Americans portrayed the Japanese as the enemy of the future. They wanted her power destroyed — even if it meant starting a preventive war.

Strength, Imperialism, and Fairness

When Roosevelt turned the presidency over to Taft in 1909, he left a legacy of strength and, he believed, fairness. Years later in his autobiography, he wrote of his role in international affairs: "During the seven and a half years that I was president, this nation behaved in international matters toward all other nations precisely as an honorable man behaves to his fellow men. We made no promise which we could not and did not keep. We made no threat which we did not carry out. We never failed to assert our rights in the face of the strong and we never failed to treat both strong and weak with courtesy and justice; and against the weak when they misbehaved we were slower to assert our rights than we were against the strong."

President Taft stood at the country's helm when a Chinese revolution overthrew the Manchu Dynasty. China began the enormous task of reorganizing and resolving her domestic problems. Taft became concerned that the Open Door policy might be violated when he saw Japan's strength at work with the building of the Hukuang Railroad through southern and central China. A Russo-Japanese railroad could easily establish for these countries an advantage over the United States in international trade. But he couldn't interest financier and railroad magnate J. P. Morgan when he proposed that U.S. and European bankers combine forces to build the international railroads.

Despite this setback, it was clear that the United States had fully emerged on to the international diplomatic stage, having stuck its imperialistic nose into problems around the world. The government negotiated, and sometimes bullied, its way into extending territories and influence, "protecting" small nations in the western hemisphere and promoting peace through demonstrated strength against Japan and Colombia.

CHAPTER 9
A Decade of Change

No one could ever have predicted that change would occur at such a rapid pace during the first decade of the twentieth century. The century had opened with a feeling of hope and promise, and by 1910, many people had realized much of that promise.

By the decade's end, previously rural landscapes had given way to huge cities with towering skyscrapers pushing the horizon. Inside the cities, factories had benefited from the scientific methods of time management, and assembly processes had been streamlined.

With the help of unions and sympathetic legislators, the country's laborers had made headway. Wages were increasing, hours were shortening, and working conditions showed signs of improvement.

By 1909, the horse and buggy had been relegated to the back of many sheds. Internal combustion engines could be heard rolling down previously quiet winding roads and above in the cloud-dappled sky. The next few years would bring many more stunning improvements in steadily developing transportation technology. Middle-income families would soon be able to afford and own one, and sometimes even two, automobiles.

A male trolley rider gets a glimpse of a lady's ankle, 1908. She is wearing a hobbleskirt, one example of the trend toward shorter skirts and less restricting corsets and petticoats. Middle-class women became more mobile in other ways during the decade, getting away from the home, joining women's clubs, and driving autos.

As the decade closed, it also promised that almost everyone would benefit from improved public transportation as trolleys and buses traveled city routes. The railroads would remain competitive through the next decade, adding passenger routes and comforts to their services. On December 5, 1909, the Pennsylvania Railroad set the world record for speed when one of its big steam locomotives was clocked at close to one hundred miles per hour.

Even the Wild West had succumbed to the changes created by the automobile. Tourism was creating a whole new industry in the West, as families packed the sedan and took road trips to see the remains of the frontier.

Faster and Better Lifestyles

It seemed that by the end of the decade, everything worked better and traveled faster. On May 10, 1909, the *Mauretania*, a ship from the Cunard cruise line, broke records on the Atlantic Ocean when it made the crossing from London to New York in four days, eighteen hours, and eleven minutes.

A year earlier, on July 1, 1908, Count Zeppelin remained aloft in his dirigible (airship) for twelve hours, crossing Switzerland at an average speed of thirty-four miles per hour. But the future clearly belonged to the airplane. The Wright brothers had continued to hold most of the air records throughout this decade and would do so well into the next.

Movie theaters gained in popularity and movie images developed more lifelike qualities, both in their film

and in their actors. Hollywood, in 1910, was on the brink of becoming the movie center of the world. It would not be long before *Theater Magazine's* daring 1908 prediction that "the time is not far distant when we will see along Broadway theatrical agencies catering to the manufacturers of moving picture films," would become reality.

The United States in 1909 was a major economic power, willing at last to acknowledge internal corruption by limiting the political power of its corporations. Its place on the world stage was set, too. America in 1909 had demonstrated that it would meet any challenge while working for global peace and economic stability.

Working-class Woes

On the home front, politicians and big business owners still held the most influence. But, under the watchful eyes of government agencies like the Department of Commerce and Labour, and under the scrutinous gaze of muckraking journalists and reformist politicians, they were no longer allowed unlimited influence.

The country had remained prosperous for the first ten years of the twentieth century. In fact, most Americans had barely noticed the Panic of 1907, the only economic downturn of the decade. J. P. Morgan negotiated with Roosevelt and created a steel monopoly to arrest an all-out depression.

But many of those who lost their jobs during the downturn were still looking for work in 1909. Records kept by the Bowery Mission estimated that every day in 1908, two thousand more needy persons stood on

"As I have said, it's sure to come. They haven't got it yet, but they will. But when the question is solved you will find that the machine that goes straight up in the air — screws itself vertically into the air — has answered the riddle."

Thomas Alva Edison, regarding the invention of helicopters

bread lines for free breakfasts of coffee and rolls. Widespread unemployment, especially of nonunion laborers, would continue into the first six months of 1909.

Meanwhile, European leaders were aligning themselves in such a way that the world's greatest conflict was about to unfold. Before that conflict would end, the United States would be drawn in and tested as a world power.

A Nation Expands

The turn of the century had marked an era when America's boundaries had reached as far west as the Pacific and as far south as Texas. It had seen the 1901 discovery of gold in California and Alaska, and the discovery of oil in Spindletop, Texas. By the end of the first decade of the twentieth century, those states and others continued to reap the harvest of those discoveries. By 1909, Texas had built a road system and developed a type of irrigation that allowed arable farming on land previously used for raising livestock. The oil and gas industry had already become firmly entrenched on Texas soil.

In 1909, the Alaska-Yukon-Pacific Exhibition in Seattle marked the expanding country's prosperity. The exhibition celebrated the fortune the Alaskan gold rush had brought to Seattle when the city became the chief outfitter for explorers and the clearing house for Alaska's fishing and other industries. The Midwest had become the manufacturing capital of the industrialized world, and the country was still growing. In 1909, there was talk in Congress of granting New Mexico

and Arizona statehood, which would make them the forty-seventh and forty-eighth states of the Union.

America had experienced tremendous change in the first decade of the twentieth century. That change affected the lives of the simplest individuals and altered the balance of world power. As financier J. P. Morgan put it, "There may be times when things are dark and cloudy in America, when uncertainty will cause some to distrust, and others to think there is too much production, too much building of railroads, and too much other enterprise. In such times, remember that the growth of this vast country will take care of all." By the end of the first decade, it appeared that the country would continue to grow. But growth and industry would not take care of all the people's needs. Rather only one thing was truly certain — as change took hold, the pace of life would continue to accelerate.

Oil was discovered at Spindletop, near Beaumont, Texas, in 1901. In 1910 the United States produced more than two hundred thousand barrels of petroleum. Its development led to prosperity for Texas and for the United States in the coming decades.

KEY DATES

1900

United States population is 75,995,000.

Cause of yellow fever is discovered in Cuba by Dr. Walter Reed and Major William Crawford Gorgas.

January 2 — First electric autostage (bus) runs in New York City.

November 3 — First auto show is held in Madison Square Garden, New York City.

1901

Oil is discovered at Spindletop, Texas.

Guglielmo Marconi sends first radio signals across the Atlantic.

February 25 — U.S. Steel Corporation is founded.

March 2 — The Platt Amendment establishes U.S. protectorate over Cuba. The amendment is accepted by Cubans in June.

March 27 — The U.S. regains control over the Philippines after three-year struggle.

September 6 — McLeon Czolgosz shoots President McKinley.

September 14 — McKinley dies and Theodore Roosevelt becomes twenty-sixth president.

October 16 — Booker T. Washington dines at the White House.

October 29 — Czolgosz is hanged.

1902

Erection of 180-foot-tall Flatiron Building is begun in New York City.

Marie and Pierre Curie isolate radium and describe its chemical properties.

July 4 — Philippine insurrection is declared over.

October 20 — Alaskan boundary dispute with Canada is settled in United States' favor.

1903

Mary "Mother" Jones leads army of children from Philadelphia to Long Island to protest the employment and exploitation of children.

Ford Motor Company is founded.

Henry James publishes *The Ambassadors*.

First transcontinental automobile trip takes place.

The Curies and colleague Henri Becquerel receive the Nobel Prize in Physics, but the Curies are too ill to make the journey to pick up the prize.

W.E.B. Du Bois publishes *The Souls of Black Folk*.

October 13 — At the first World Series, Boston beat Pittsburgh.

November 3 — Panama rebels against Colombia with U.S. help.

November 6 — United States recognizes Panama's independence.

November 19 — The Hay-Bunau-Varilla Treaty with Panama permits the United States to build the Panama Canal.

December 17 — The first airplane flight is made by the Wright Brothers at Kitty Hawk, North Carolina.

1904

Frank Lloyd Wright completes the Larkin Building in Buffalo.

Mary McLeod Bethune founds the Daytona Normal School and Industrial Institute for Negro Girls in Daytona, Florida.

Ida Tarbell publishes *The History of the Standard Oil Company*.

February 8 — Russo-Japanese War begins when Japan surprises the Russians at Port Arthur.

May 9 — Construction of the Panama Canal begins.

October 27 — New York City subway opens.

December 6 — The Roosevelt Corollary to the Monroe Doctrine is announced.

1905

Immigration to the United States reaches an annual peak over the next three years of 3,400,000.

Einstein publishes a research paper on his "Theory of Relativity."

The Niagara Movement, headed by W.E.B. Du Bois, campaigns for racial equality.

June — The Industrial Workers of the World (the IWW, or "Wobblies") is formed.

September 5 — A peace treaty, mediated by U.S. President Theodore Roosevelt, at Portsmouth, New Hampshire, ends the Russo-Japanese War.

1906

Hostility toward African-Americans leads to riots in Brownsville, Texas, and Atlanta, Georgia.

Upton Sinclair publishes *The Jungle*.

April 18 — San Francisco shakes with an earthquake. The subsequent fire burns over 2,800 acres of the city.

September 24 — Roosevelt designates the Devil's Tower a National Monument.

December 10 — Roosevelt is awarded the Nobel Peace Prize for ending the Russo-Japanese War.

1907

Every southern state has laws against integration.

Panic of 1907 begins with a stock market crash.

January 27 — Metropolitan Opera House withdraws Strauss's *Salome* after it is denounced as immoral.

March 14 — Immigration Act makes it possible for immigrants without U.S. passports to be barred from entry to the country if it is deemed detrimental to American labor conditions.

November 16 — Oklahoma enters the Union as the forty-sixth state.

December 16 — The Great White Fleet begins world tour.

1908

The Model T Ford is produced as the first affordable automobile.

"The Eight" open an independent display of paintings at the Macbeth Gallery, New York City.

June 8 — The National Conservation Commission is established.

1909

The National Association for the Advancement of Colored People is created.

Wright Brothers form the Wright Company to produce airplanes commercially.

April 6 — Robert E. Peary and Matthew A. Henson reach the North Pole.

May 3 — A wireless telegraphic press message sent from New York to Chicago.

September 10 — Freud and Jung start American tour.

By the end of 1909, the U.S. population reaches 91,972,266.

FURTHER READING

Asimov, Isaac. *The Golden Door: The United States from 1865 to 1918.* Boston: Houghton Mifflin Company, 1977.

Barck, Theodore, Jr. and Nelson Manfred Blake. *Since 1900: A History of the United States in Our Times*, 4th ed. New York: The MacMillian Company, 1965.

Bennett, Lerone Jr. *Pioneers in Protest.* Chicago: Johnson Publishing Company, 1968.

Berkin, Carol Ruth and Mary Beth Norton. *Women of America.* Boston: Houghton Mifflin Company, 1979.

Brownlow, Kevin and John Kobol. *Hollywood: The Pioneers.* New York: Alfred A. Knopf, 1979.

Forster, Margaret. *Significant Sisters: The Grassroots of Active Feminism, 1839-1939.* New York: Alfred A. Knopf, 1985.

Freedman, Russell. *The Wright Brothers: How They Invented the Airplane.* New York: Holiday House, 1991.

Garraty, John A. *Theodore Roosevelt: The Strenuous Life.* New York: American Heritage Publishing, 1967.

Ingraham, Claire R. and Leonard Ingraham. *An Album of Women in American History.* New York: Franklin Watts, 1972.

James, Portia P. *The Real McCoy: African-American Invention and Innovation, 1619-1930.* Washington: Smithsonian Institution Press, 1989.

Link, William A. and Arthur S. Link. *The Twentieth Century: An American History.* Arlington Heights, Illinois: Harlan Davidson, Inc., 1983.

Lord, Walter. *The Good Years From 1900 to the First World War.* New York: Harper & Brothers Publishers, 1960.

McKissack, Patricia and Frederick McKissack. *The Civil Rights Movement in America from 1865 to Present.* Chicago: Childrens Press, 1987.

Roosevelt, Theodore. *The Autobiography of Theodore Roosevelt.* New York: Charles Scribner's Sons, 1958.

Schudson, Michael. *Discovering the News: A Social History of American Newspapers.* New York: Basic Books, Inc., 1973.

Smith, Page. *America Enters the World: A People's History of the Progressive Era and World War I.* Vol 7. New York: McGraw-Hill Book Company, 1985.

Trager, James, ed. *The People's Chronology.* New York: Henry Holt Company, 1992.

Wood, Walter et al., eds. *200 Years of American Worklife.* Washington, D.C: U.S. Department of Labor, Employment and Training Administrations, 1977.

INDEX

Adams, Maude, 115, *115*
Addams, Jane, 46–47, *48*
Adler, Alfred, 94
African-Americans: image in popular culture, 52; segregation, 30, 36–37; suffrage, 36–37; violence against, 30, 37–38
Agriculture, 97, 98
Airplanes, 102–6, *104, 105, 106*
Airships, 136
Alaska, 126, 130
Alexander's Bridge (Cather), 112
The Ambassadors (James), 112
American Automobile Association, 108
American Federation of Labor, 75
American Foundation for Overseas Blind, 113
American Foundation for the Blind, 113
American Indians, 23, 42–44, *42*
Americanization, 45
Anthony, Susan B., 30, 31
Anti-imperialism, 125–27
The Appeal to the Great Spirit (Dallin), 119–20
Architecture, 121–23
Arizona, 137
Ash Can School, 118
Atlanta, Georgia, 40
Automobiles, 106–10, *107, 108*

Baer, George F., 74
Baker, Ray Stannard, 37
Ballinger, Richard A., 82
Barnard, George Grey, 121
Barnett, Ida Bell Wells. See Wells-Barnett, Ida Bell
Barrie, J.M., 115
Barrymore, Ethel, 115
Baseball, 60–63
Becquerel, Henri, 96
Bell, Alexander Graham, 113
Bellows, George, 118
Ben Hur, 57–58
Benz, Karl, 106
Berlin, Irving, 58
Bernhardt, Sarah, 115
Bethune, Mary McLeod, 88, **91**, *91*
Bill Bailey Won't You Please Come Home, 52
Bleriot, Louis, 105, 106
Blues, 58–59
Borden, Gail, 101
Boutwell, George, 126
Boxing, 63

Bras d'Or Lake, Nova Scotia, 105
Bronco-buster (Remington), *120*
Brownsville, Texas, 38
Bryan, William Jennings, 77, 125
Buffalo Bill, 54
Buffalo, New York, 70; Larkin Building, 122
Bunau-Varilla, Philippe, 129
Burnham, Daniel E., 122, *123*
Burns, Tommy, 63
Business: power over government, 26–27, 70–72; trusts, 76–79, *77*, 89
Buster Brown, 66

California, 126
The Call of the Wild (London), 114
Camille, 115
Canada, 130
Cantor, Eddie, 52
Captain Jinks of the Horse Marines, 115
Carnegie Institute, 87
Carnegie, Andrew, 72, 87, *88*, 113
Cartoons, newspaper, 66
Carver, George Washington, 97, **98**, *98*
Cather, Willa, 112
Central America. *See* Latin America and specific countries
Cézanne, Paul, 116
Chicago, 47, 59–60
Child labor, 27, 48–49, *49*
China, 134
Chinese Exclusion Act (1882), 30
Churchill, Winston (writer), 112
Clark, M.B., 89
Classical music, 59
Cleveland, Grover, 36, 125
Cobb, Ty, 60–62, **61**, *61*
Coeur d'Alene, Idaho, 75
Cohan, George M., 115
Colombia, 129–30
Come Josephine, in My Flying Machine, 52
Constitutional amendments: Fourteenth Amendment, 36–37
Correns, Carl, 93
Corruption in business and politics, *26*, 27
The Count of Monte Cristo, 57–58
Crocker, Sewall K., 107
Cuba, 90–93, 126–28
Cubism, 117
Cunard, 111, 136
Curie, Marie, 95–96, *95*
Curie, Pierre, 95–96
Curtiss, Glenn, 105
Czolgosz, McLeon, 69–70

Dallin, Edwin Cyrus, 119–20

Dance, 124
The Darktown Strutters Ball, 52
Darwin, Charles, 71–72
Davies, Arthur B., 118
Dawes Act (1887), 44
Dayton, Ohio, 102–3
Daytona, Florida, 88, 91
De Mille, Cecil B., 56
Debs, Eugene V., 72–73
Degas, Edgar, 116
Department stores, 24, *25*
Diesel, Rudolf, 111
Diesel engine, 111
Dr. Jekyll and Mr. Hyde, 115
A Doll's House (Ibsen), 116
Domestic appliances, 97–99, *99*
Drago Doctrine, 131
Drama, 115–16
Dreiser, Theodore, 112
Du Bois, W.E.B., 30, 40, 41–42, **41**, *41*
Dunbar, Paul Laurence, 114, **114**, *114*
Duncan, Isadora, 124, **124**, *124*

Eakins, Thomas, 119
Eastman, George, 120
Edison, Thomas Alva, 54, *54*, **55**, *55*
Ehrlich, Paul, 93
The Eight, 118
Einstein, Albert, 96, *96*
Elektra (Strauss), 59
Elkins Act (1903), 80
Environmental conservation, 82, 83–85
European imperialism, 125. *See also* specific countries
Expressionism, 116, 124
Exultations (Pound), 115

The Faith Healer (Moody), 116
Fashion, 34, *34*, 50, *135*
Federal Children's Bureau, 49, 88
Fetch, Tom, 107
Field, Marshall, 24, 25
Finley, Carlos J., 90, 92
Fisher, H.C. "Bud," 66
Flagg, Ernest, 122
Flink, James J., 108
Following the Color Line (Baker), 37
Food and Drug Act (1906), 81
Food industry, 81–83, 100–101, *101*
Football, 63, *64*
Ford, Henry, 26, 109–10
Ford Motors: Model T, 109–10, *109*
Fort Myers, Virginia, 105
Foy, Eddie, 60
Fred Ott's Sneeze, 54
French, Daniel Chester, 121

Freud, Sigmund, 93–95, *94*

Gamble, J.G., 88, 91
Gauguin, Paul, 116
Geronimo, **43**, *43*
Gibson Girls, 120, *120*
Gibson, Charles Dana, 120, *120*
Glackens, William, 118
Goethals, George, 130
The Golden Bowl (James), 112
Gompers, Samuel, 46, 75
Gorgas, William Crawford, 90–93
The Governor's Son (Cohan), 115
Grant, Ulysses S., 44
Great Britain, 132
The Great Divide (Moody), 116
The Great Train Robbery, 56–57, *57*
Griffith, D.W., 57
Guitar (Picasso), *117*

Hales Tours and Scenes of the World, 57
Hammond, Eugene, 107–8
Hanna, Mark, 69, 70, **71**, *71*
Happy Hooligan, 66
Hawthorne, Charles, 118
Hay, John, 125, 129
Hay-Bunau-Varilla Treaty (1903), 129
Haywood, William "Big Bill" Dudley, **75**, *75*
Health, 86, 88
Hearst, William Randolph, 65–66
Hello Ma Baby (Joplin), 58
Henri, Robert, 118
Henson, Matthew A., 84, **85**, *85*
Highland Park, Illinois: Willets House, 122
Hill, James Jerome, 77
Hine, Lewis, *45*, *49*
Hobart, Garret, 68
Hollywood, California, 54–56, 136
Homer, Winslow, 118–19, *119*
Homestead Act (1862), 22
Hopkins, Frederick G., 88
Housing, 23, *48*
Howells, William Dean, 112
Hulbert, William, 63

Ibsen, Henrik, 116
Immigration Act (1907), 47
Immigration, *29*; from Asia, 30; from Japan, 133; from N & W Europe, 29–30, 46; from S & E Europe, 44–47, *45*
Imperialism: European, 125; U.S., 125–31, 134
Impressionism, 116
In My Merry Oldsmobile, 52

In the Good Old Summertime, 58
Industrial Workers of the World (IWW), 75–76
The Interpretation of Dreams (Freud), 94
The Iron Heel (London), 114

Jackson, H. Nelson, 107
James, Frank, 53
James, Henry, 112
James, Jesse, 53
Japan, 132–34
Jeffries, James J., 63
Jim Crow laws, 36
Johnson, Jack, 63, *63*
Jones, Mary Harris "Mother," 27, **28**, *28*, 48–49
Joplin, Scott, 58
Journalism. *See* Magazines; Newspapers
Jung, Carl Gustav, 94–95, *94*
The Jungle (Sinclair), 81–82

Katsura (Prime Minister), 133
The Katzenjammer Kids, 66
Keller, Helen, 112, **113**, *113*
Kelley, Florence, 27
Kellogg, Will Keith, 100–101
Keppler, Joseph, *26*
Kinetoscope, 54, *54*
Kitty Hawk, North Carolina, 102–3
Kodak cameras, 120, *121*
Korea, 133
Ku Klux Klan, 37, 91

La Follette, Robert Marion, Sr., 67, 72, **73**, *73*
Labor movement, 74–76, 80. *See also* Strikes
Lacey Act (1900), 83
Ladenburg, Mrs. Adolph, 34
Lamb, Charles R., 36
Larkin Building, Buffalo, New York, 122
Latin America, 125, 126, 130–31. *See also* specific countries
Le Brun, Napoleon, 123
Lee, Ivy, 65
Lilienthal, Otto, 102
Lindsay, Vachel, 86
Literature, 112–15
Little Napoleon. *See* McGraw, John J.
Lodge, Henry Cabot, 125
London, Jack, 112–14, *112*
Luks, George, 118, *118*
Lusitania, 111

McClure's, 66
McCurdy, John A.D., 105

McDonald, John B., 110
McGraw, John J., 60
Mack, Connie, 60
McKinley, William, 68, 69–70, 71, 132; and Cuba, 126–28
Macy, John, 113
Madame Butterfly (Puccini), 59
Magazines, 63–65, *65*, 66–67, 80–81
Majors and Minors (Dunbar), 114
Mansfield, Richard, 115
Maple Leaf Rag (Joplin), 58
Marconi, Guglielmo, 53
Martin, John B., 50
Marx, Karl, 29
Mathewson, Christy, 60
Mauretania, 111, *111*, 136
Meat Inspection Act (1906), 82–83
Medicine, 87, 90–93, *90*
Melies, Georges, 56
The Melting Pot (Zangwill), 116
Mendel, Gregor Johann, 93
Merrill, David, 53
Miles, Harry H., 56
Mrs. Warren's Profession (Shaw), 115–16
Mitchell, John, 74
Monet, Claude, 116
Monroe Doctrine, 126, 130
Moody, William Vaughn, 116
Morgan, John Pierpont, 25, 77, **78**, *78*, 79, *79*, 132, 134, 137
Morgan, Julius, 78
Mott, Lucretia, 31
Movies, 53–58, 136
Muckrakers, 66, 80–81
Munch, Edvard, 116
Muscle Shoals, Alabama, 84
Music. *See* Blues; Classical music; Popular music; Ragtime
Mutt and Jeff, 66, *66*

Nation, 66
Nation, Carry, 30, 35, *35*
National Association for the Advancement of Colored People (NAACP), 41
National Conference of Charities and Corrections, 46–47
National Negro Business League, 40
National Woman Suffrage Association, 30
A Negro Explorer at the North Pole (Henson), 85
The Negro in Business (Washington), 40
Nevada, 126
New Mexico, 137
New York City, *22*, 87, 110; Coney Island, 67; Ellis Island, 44–45, *45*;

Page numbers in *italic* indicate picture; page numbers in **bold** indicate biography

Flatiron building, 122, *123*;
Metropolitan Life Tower, 123;
Pennsylvania Station, 123; Pierpont
Morgan Library, 123; Singer Building,
122; Woolworth Building, 121
Newlands Reclamation Act (1902), 83
Newspapers, 63–66
Nickelodeons, *56*, 57
North Pole, first men at, 84, 85
The North Pole (Peary), 85
Northern Securities Company, 77, 78
Northward Over the "Great Ice"
(Peary), 85

O'Keeffe, Georgia, 122
Oak Park, Illinois: Unity Church, 122
Oakley, Annie, 54
Oil industry in Texas, 137, *137*
Olds, Ransom Eli, 106
Open Door policy, 126
Orchard, Harry, 75
Organ, Marjorie, 118
Osborn, H.F., 46
Outlook, 66

Panama, 129–30
Panama Canal, 110, 126, 129–30,
129, 134
Parker, Alton B., 80
Parsifal (Wagner), 59
Parsons, Charles A., 110–11
Pasteur, Louis, 88
Peary, Robert Edwin, 84, **85**, *85*
Pelican Island, Florida, 83
Personal (Pound), 115
Peter Pan (Barrie), 115, *115*
Philippines, 128–29
Phonographs, 51
Photography, 120–21, *121*
Picasso, Pablo, 116–17
Pickford, Mary, 58
Pierce, Sir William H., 53
Pinchot, Gifford, *82*, 82, 83, 84
Platt Amendment (1901), 127
Popular music, 51, 52, 58
Populism, 72
Porter, Edwin S., 56–57
Portsmouth, Treaty of (1905), 132
Pound, Ezra, 115
Poverty, urban, 27, 46–49, *47*, *48*, 87
Prendergast, Maurice, 118
Presidential elections: of 1900, 68–69; of
1904, 80; of 1908, 84
Printing, 63–64
Progressive, 67, 73
Progressivism, 72, 77
Prohibition, 30, 35, 50

Psychology, 93–95
Public transportation, 110, *110*, 136
Puccini, Giacomo, 59
Pulitzer, Joseph, 65–66

Radio, 53
Radioactivity, 95–97
Ragtime, 58
Railroads, *33*, 77, 79, 110, 136
Rebecca of Sunnybrook Farm (Wiggin), 112
Reed, Thomas, 125
Reed, Walter, 90–92, **92**, *92*, 93
Remington, Frederic, 119;
Bronco-buster, *120*
Renoir, Auguste, 116
Rescued from an Eagle's Nest, 57
Richard Carvel (Churchill), 112
Richards, Ellen, 50
Rockefeller Foundation, 87, 89
Rockefeller, John D., 77, 79, 87, 88, **89**,
89, 91
Rogers, W.A., 77, *128*
Rogers, Will, 52, 60, *60*
Roosevelt Corollary, 130–31
Roosevelt Dam, Arizona, 83, *83*
Roosevelt, Theodore J., 22, 38, *68*,
69–70, 71, 82, 88, 127; and 1900
election, 68–69; and 1904 election, 80,
80; and 1912 election, 72; and big
business, 76–79, *77*; and child labor,
28, 49, 73–74; and Japan, 132–34, *133*;
and Panama, 129–30, *129*, *130*;
domestic policies, 39–40, 45, 47,
74–75, 80, *80*, 81–84; foreign policy,
125, *128*, 130–31, 134
Root, Elihu, 131, **132**, *132*, 134
Rubell, Ira, 64
Russia, 126, 132–33
Rutherford, Ernest, 97
Ryder, Albert Pinkham, 119

Saint-Gaudens, Augustus, 121
St. Louis, 52–53, *52*
Salome (Strauss), 59, *59*
San Francisco, 133; earthquake,
108–9, *109*
Sargent, Aaron A., 31
Sargent, John Singer, 117
School Days, 58
Sea Wolf (London), 114
Sears Roebuck and Co., 30, *32*
Seattle, 137
Selfridge, Thomas E., 105
Settlement of the West, 22–23, 53
Shaw, George Bernard, 115–16
Shinn, Everett, 118
Shipping, 110–11, *111*

Shoshone Dam, Wyoming, 83
Sinclair, Upton, 81–82
Sister Carrie (Dreiser), 112
Sloan, John, *56*, 118
Smith, Hamilton E., 98
Social Darwinism, 71–72
The Song of the Stone Wall (Keller), 113
Song pluggers, 58
The Souls of Black Folk (Du Bois), 40
Spalding, Albert Goodwill, **62**, *62*, 63
Spencer, Herbert, 72
Spindletop, Texas, 137, *137*
The Sport of the Gods (Dunbar), 114
Sport, 60–63
Springfield, Illinois, 40
The Squaw Man, 56
Standard Oil Company, 79, 89
Stanton, Elizabeth Cady, 30, **31**, *31*
Starr, Ellen Gates, 46–47
Steam turbine, 110–11
Steffens, Lincoln, 81
Steichen, Edward, 121, 122
Steunenberg, Frank, 75
Stevens, John F., 130
Stieglitz, Alfred, 121, **122**, *122*
Stiles, Wardell, 87
The Story of My Life (Keller), 113
Strauss, Richard, 59
Strikes: coal (1902), 74; Coeur d'Alene,
Idaho (1899), 75
Sullivan Ordinance (1909), 50
Sullivan, Anne, 113
Sumner, William Graham, 72
Supreme Court cases: *Plessy v. Ferguson*
(1896), 30
Sweet Adeline, 58

Taft, Lorado, 121
Taft, William Howard, 82, 84–85, 128,
131, 133
Takahira, Kogoro, 132, 134
Tarbell, Ida, 81, *81*
Taylor, Frederick W., **100**, *100*,
101, 110
Tennessee Coal and Iron Company
(TC & I), 79, 132
Tracy, Harry, 53
Tschermak, Erich, 93
Tuskegee Institute, 39, *39*, 40
Twain, Mark, 112, 129
Tweed, William M., 27

Under the Bamboo Tree (Joplin), 58
Unemployment, 136–37
United Mine Workers, 74
Unity Church, Oak Park, Illinois, 122
Up From Slavery (Washington), 40, 66

Page numbers in *italic* indicate picture; page numbers in **bold** indicate biography

Urbanization, 24–25, 86–87
U.S. Steel Corporation, 79, 132
Utah, 126

Van Gogh, Vincent, 116
Varilla, Philippe Bunau.
 See Bunau-Varilla, Philippe
Vaudeville, 52, 59–60
The Virginian (Wister), 120
Visual arts, 116–20, 121
Vries, Hugo, 93

Wagner, Richard, 59
Wait, Pearl, 100
Wald, Lillian, 49, 88
Walker Law (1920), 63
Washington, Booker T., 30, 39, 40, **40**,
 40, 41–42, 66, 91
Waters Pierce Oil Company, 89
The Way of the Indian (Remington), 119
Wells-Barnett, Ida Bell, 38, *38*
Whistler, James McNeill, 116
White, Thomas H., 91
White, William Allen, 132
Whitman, L.L., 107–8
Wiggin, Kate Douglas, 112
Wiley, Harvey W., 81
Willets House, Highland Park,
 Illinois, 122
Williams, William Carlos, 114–15
Wilson, Emma, 91
The Wings of the Dove (James), 112
Winton, Alexander, 106
Wister, Owen, 120
Wobblies. *See* Industrial Workers of
 the World
Women: in society, 36, 50, *108*, 135. *See
 also* Fashion
Women's movement: suffrage, 30, 35, 49,
 50
The World We Live In (Keller), 113
World's Work, 67
Wright, Frank Lloyd, 121–22
Wright, Orville, 102–5, **103**, *103*, *104*
Wright, Wilbur, 102–5, **103**, *103*

Yellow fever, 90–93
Yellow journalism, 66
Young, Cy, 60

Zangwill, Israel, 116
Zeppelin, Count, 136

ACKNOWLEDGMENTS

The author and publishers wish to thank the following for
permission to reproduce copyright material:

The Bettmann Archive: *frontispiece*, 22, 23, 26, 28, 31, 32,
34, 39, 40, 41, 45, 48 (upper and lower), 49, 51, 52, 54,
55, 57, 59, 62, 63, 65, 68, 71, 77, 78, 79, 80, 81, 82, 83,
85 (upper and lower), 87, 90, 91, 92, 94, 96, 98, 99, 100,
101, 103, 104, 108, 109 (both), 110, 111, 112, 115, 117,
119, 120 (lower), 121, 124, 130, 132, 133, 134, 137;
Bettmann Newsphotos: 56; Culver Pictures Inc: 50, 67,
85 (lower), 114; The Granger Collection, New York: 29,
55, 74, 75, 128; Peter Newark's American Pictures: 25,
33, 42, 60, 64, 73, 88, 105, 106, 107, 118, 120 (upper),
127, 129; Pach/Bettmann: 89; UPI/Bettmann: 35, 38, 43,
61, 113, 122, 123, 135.

The illustrations on pages 24, 25, 46, and 76 are by Rafi
Mohammed.

Page numbers in *italic* indicate picture; page numbers in **bold** indicate biography